A Taste for

Language

A Recipe for Second Language Acquisition

by Mary Jo Ervin

Melting Pot Press
P.O. Box 2005
Howell, Michigan 48844

i

The illustrations within the text were done by Rebecca Streby.

Printed in the United States of America.

First Edition.
Library of Congress Catalog No. 88-092521

ISBN 0-9621272-0-5

Order direct from the publisher.

TABLE OF CONTENTS

- Translations in this work may not be exact.
- To avoid the constant use of he/she the author has elected to use "he" when referring to the child. "She" is used to refer to the teacher.

ACKNOWLEDGMENTS

I would like to gratefully recognize the following people and organizations for their valuable contributions to this work.

Staff of Livingston Montessori, Brighton, MI, whose hard word and dedication inspired this work.

Ferndale Public Schools, MI, particulary Lynn Haire, Irma Torres, Annick Brown and Barbara Abel for sharing their classroom expertise with me and whose original ideas appear throughout this work.

Dr. James J. Asher whose comments and advice regarding the manuscript were appreciated.

Joe Moore, master teacher and editor of *DORS to Language.*
Jenni Kotarski, master teacher and contributor to this work.
Gene Lynch, master teacher and co-author of **The Zoo and Other Things to Do.**
Jan Keenan, Lita Bustillo, Ramiro Garcia, Myriam Met, Maggie D'Allemand.

Carol Chen for her assistance in distributing and collecting completed questionnaires from bilingual parents.

Huguette Piha for her insight into the bilingual experience at home and in the Montessori classroom.

Nelida Mietta-Fontana, Cincinnati Public Schools, for her gracious hospitality while visiting the Bilingual Academy and other schools using partial immersion.

Eileen DeBurton for her assistance in editing and translation.
Mrs. Nan Monroe, Jenny Seim and Margie Gerulski (music composition).
Diana Seim for her assistance in proofreading and translation.
Pam Gingerich and Katherine Pfeffer Chouinard (initial artwork).
Rebecca Streby, whose wonderful sketches capture a child's world.
Joan Keely, my right hand during this project, whose organizational and typesetting expertise is without peer.
G-Graphics, Brighton, MI (producer).

HP Books, Inc. for recipes reprinted from **Mexican Cookery**.

Betty Burton
Friends, family and teachers who believed in my ability.
My children, Annie, Julie and Joan whose curiosity and anticipation nudged this work to completion, and
My husband, Mike, whose patience and enthusiasm encouraged me to succeed.

PREFACE

Language is the spice of life. Or so children have discovered. From the time they are very young, children communicate with those around them. Their goal is to be understood. And so it is with adults. We were all once children and now may find ourselves communicating a second language to our offspring or students.

Whether you are a bilingual parent, a pre-school foreign language teacher, or an elementary teacher of foreign language, this book is for you! You have acquired a "taste" for language and are anxious to share it with children. Some of you are thinking: Where do I begin? What do I teach? How do I motivate children to learn another language?

This work is the result of school observations both in the state of Michigan and out of state. Foreign language programs were observed in public and private settings in Grand Rapids, Lansing, Flint, Ann Arbor, Ferndale, Troy, Birmingham, and Dearborn, Michigan. Cincinnati and Tiffin Schools provided the out of state observations. My research also includes responses from questionnaires sent to bilingual parents in the Washington, D.C. area. These parents are involved in promoting a second language at home and at Saturday schools, which their children attend.

The experiences outlined in **A Taste for Language** are common to many foreign language teachers. This work consolidates the best teaching applications and condenses them for easy reference.

The activities illustrated in **A Taste for Language** can be used with toddlers and elementary aged children. Some high school foreign language teachers may even find the activities both meaningful and applicable for their first year students. Finally, bilingual parents who are teaching at home may find this book a valuable resource in whetting their child's appetite for acquiring a second language.

Twenty-two topics have been developed in the body of the book for your enjoyment and application. While the topics have been ordered, they need not follow a sequenced curriculum. The beauty of the activities is that they can be combined to fill a particular time frame and need not require a 30-40 minute class. The activities can enhance an already existing program. They may also form the basis of programs using shorter intervals of exposure to the language.

A Taste for Language will streamline your work as a language teacher. It will offer you a proven method to use for teaching foreign language to young children. It will provide you "recipes for success" by way of games, songs, fingerplays, cooking, culture capsules, and reinforcement activities. For simplicity's sake, the recipes are in English. However, specific commands and vocabulary are in a target language, in this case, Spanish. The Spanish translation is identified by *italics* and the recipes or lessons are easily adapted to other languages.

A Taste for Language will teach you how to create a stress-free environment where children will flourish and be excited about communicating in another language. You will learn how to evaluate the child's progress . . . And you will see the child succeed.

One final note. You have made a foreign language commitment. You are armed with the powerful wisdom of many teachers before you. Go ahead. Taste a second language the child's way and savor the results!

To my husband, Mike, who uses language every day . . .
and people feel good.

To my daughters, Annie, Julie and Joan, who make
our house a home.

Children are fascinated by the new sounds they are hearing and will try very hard to discern meaning from them.

Children are naturally curious about different sounds.

Young children by nature are excellent mimics. They delight in role play and can adopt the behavior and speech mannerisms of a teacher or parent.

Children enjoy imitating others and therefore develop good listening habits and correct pronunciation.

CHAPTER I
Why a Foreign Language So Young?

Whether you are a bilingual parent or a schoolteacher you will undoubtedly be influencing those around you by your decision to promote a foreign language at home or school. People will be curious as to why you decided to pursue this goal, how you go about teaching foreign language to young children and what the results are. With this in mind I would like to outline various reasons for teaching a foreign language to children. Keep in mind that this outline might also serve as a topic for a parent newsletter home or a parents night presentation.

When considering foreign language acquisition in young children the question arises, "Why so young?"

Those who start second languages as children can reach higher levels of competence because of the opportunities they have had. It appears that the longer the period of exposure and interaction in a foreign language the greater the likelihood that the child will become fluent in the language. Acquisition will depend on a number of variables which will be discussed in Chapter II. However, for introductory purposes, we know that the value of studying a foreign language cannot be underestimated. The sooner we begin, the better.

It is my experience that small children by a large margin enjoy learning a foreign language. Movement and manipulation of objects are natural behaviors for them.

Foreign language learning is enjoyable.

Young children are less self-conscious about pronouncing strange sounds than are adolescents. Oftentimes I hear children repeating a new word aloud even though I am satisfied that they listen first. I have seen children use the foreign language to help other children understand.

Children are less self-conscious about pronouncing strange words.

Children are accustomed to repetition and drill. They delight in repeating and fast become proud of their counting ability in the language.

Children are accustomed to repetition and drill.

Because of their natural ability to imitate, their curiosity with new sounds, and consistent practice, young children acquire good pronunciation skills.

Children who begin second language learning early and continue it, develop good listening habits and sound discrimination skills. As a result, they can become better readers in their native language. Research conducted in Canada shows improvement for foreign language students in mathematics and in English vocabulary and reading. Much later, when grammar is introduced, children will understand the mechanics of their own language better after having used a second language.

Children who begin second language early have an increased awareness and understanding of their own language.

Studying a foreign language at a young age offers information to children that is being absorbed at a phenomenal rate. Children, particularly from the ages of 2-1/2 to 5, are like sponges. Children enjoy correlating the new language with other areas of the school curriculum. In a Montessori classroom, for example, young children delight in using the color tablets, blue/ red rods, metal insets and large wooden maps of continents because they are already familiar with them. Foreign language offers a new dimension to using these materials.

*Children enjoy correlating the study of a foreign language
with other areas of the school curriculum.*

Another advantage for the young child of foreign language study is gaining an early cultural awareness of a language and the people who speak it. Children are intrigued by different clothing, customs, food, lifestyles and even names! I remember one occasion when the children were sending small gifts to a boy in Honduras. His name was Marlon. Apparently Michael Jackson's brother has the same name. The children wanted to know if this boy Marlon was a relative of Michael Jackson's brother! In this instance the children found great joy in equating their existing knowledge of the world with the knowledge they were recently acquiring.

Children gain an early cultural awareness of the foreign language and its people.

Children become comfortable using a second language and can apply it in real-life situations. The new language becomes second nature to them because of consistent and meaningful exposure.

Children develop a feeling of "at homeness" with the second language.

Finally, a longer sequence of language study is beneficial to children personally and professionally. Second language acquisition provides a broad, creative basis upon which to live, work, and appreciate in this world.

A longer sequence of language study is beneficial to children.

The following excerpt from "A Nation at Risk" Report of the National Commission on Excellence in Education, April, 1983 summarizes the value of foreign language study.

"Achieving proficiency in a foreign language ordinarily requires from four to six years of study, and, therefore, should be started in the elementary grades. We believe it is desirable that students achieve such proficiency because study of a foreign language introduces the student to non-English speaking cultures, heightens awareness and comprehension of one's native tongue and serves the nation's needs in commerce, diplomacy, defense and education."

CHAPTER II
Principles that Promote

Second language acquisition and second language learning are separate but integral components of foreign language study. A distinction between the two necessarily involves a brief discussion of the brain.

Perhaps one of the greatest breakthroughs in the field of education involves the realization that for optimum learning to take place both hemispheres of the brain need to be used. Brain research is applicable in all subject areas but particularly in second language acquisition.

The human brain houses two hemispheres. The right hemisphere is mute. The artistic or picture and physical response appeal to this area of the brain. The left hemisphere talks. Words or speech and logic appeal to this area of the brain. Both hemispheres are continually monitoring one another. Both hemispheres are tapped in foreign language learning.

Let us consider the characteristics of persons whose right brain is dominant. Right brain learners have random thought patterns, intuition, a love of fantasy, a holistic view of life and non-verbal skills. Right-brained children may often appear restless and concentration is difficult for them. Techniques which activate the right brain include the following:

1. manipulating objects; hands-on activities.
2. problem-solving through pattern recognition, intuition or guessing.
3. looking for similarities and connections.
4. thinking in images.
5. artwork, drama, dance, music, movement, role-playing.
6. brainstorming.
7. engaging the senses, involve the emotions.

The left brain learner on the other hand, is characterized by good verbal abilities, logical and sequential thinking and a realistic approach to life. Traditionally, formal education has addressed the person whose left brain was dominant. The following techniques apply to left brain learners:

1. teacher demonstrates and/or lectures.
2. looking for differences and distinctions.
3. language is relied on in thinking, learning and memory functions.
4. reading, writing and talking.
5. sequential and time-ordered processing activities.
6. verbalization and computation.
7. problem-solving that emphasizes finding "the" correct answer.

As we have noted, foreign language teaching involves the activation of both brain hemispheres. Communicative and non-communicative activities each play a role in foreign language learning. Traditional approaches to foreign language teaching have relied heavily on non-communicative activities for fluency. Current foreign language theory emphasizes the need for communicative activities to achieve fluency. A careful examination of the distinction between the two kinds of activities will be helpful in promoting a successful foreign language program at home or in school.

Communicative activities involve the following:

1. interacting extemporaneously in the foreign language to express greetings, introductions and pleasantries.
2. filling the information gap between speakers.
3. role-playing ad-lib roles in real life situations.
4. initiating language and responses appropriate in real-life situations.
5. giving or receiving instructions or explanations.
6. using language to describe situations or to express needs and feelings.
7. cycling and recycling of newly learned words and idioms in authentic contexts.
8. writing and reading messages.

Non-communicative activities on the other hand involve the following:

1. memorization and reciting dialogues.
2. translating.
3. performing substitution drills.
4. answering questions with pre-determined answers.
5. pronunciation exercises.
6. writing dictation.
7. written drills.
8. singing or reciting poetry.
9. explaining the concept or word in English.
10. completing fill-in exercises.
11. rearranging sentences.

Second language **acquisition** then refers to the principle that languages are "caught not taught." Acquisition is a right brain process which occurs through a period of listening and interaction in the new language over time. Movement or physical response accelerates the acquisition process. Speech emerges spontaneously because it is purposeful and of personal significance. It is not rehearsed, directed or repeated. It is free.

Second language **learning** generally refers to left-brain work such as grammar, translation and drill. Rules of reading, writing, and talking are emphasized.

A Taste for Language includes both communicative (right-brain) and non-communicative (left-brain) approaches to foreign language. The emphasis however, is on communication. Young children in particular enjoy physical movement and repetition and drill. Both approaches satisfy the child's taste for language.

A communicative approach to foreign language teaching is designed with specific student expectations or incentives for learning in mind. Consider the following expectations of the children:

1. immediate gratification; feedback from the teacher.
2. active participation of the child in a game or activity right from the start even if the child is awkward at first.
3. child is satisfied in knowing that he can understand and/or use the foreign language better than the week before.
4. language practice is interesting and meaningful.
5. child sees language experience as purposeful for personal growth.

Once the child's incentives for learning have been identified the teacher or parent can concentrate on the method. One such method which is highly successful with small children is the Total Physical Response or TPR method. TPR originated with Dr. James Asher of San Jose State University, California. Dr. Asher has over twenty years of research and practical experience to support the TPR application. His method is based on the concept that children and adults assimilate a second language first through the body. Infants spend their first two years of life listening to and watching those around them. They learn by associating physical action and tangible objects to spoken words. Infants are given much encouragement as they first begin to speak and their language is accepted in the form that it is spoken. Much later fine tuning of their native language occurs when the child can accept criticism with a minimum of fear and stress. Reading follows a long period of hearing the spoken word.

Children in their first years of foreign language exposure are asked to listen to commands such as "Stand up," "Sit down," etc. They demonstrate their comprehension by performing the appropriate action. The physical action triggers and solidifies the acquisition process. Total Physical Response is used to teach a variety of tenses such as: "By the time I count to five you will have gone to the board, written your name and sat down in your seat." Commands are recombined and an infinite variety of vocabulary ensues. An element of surprise is critical to teaching this method of foreign language as it heightens enthusiasm and comradery in the classroom.

The benefits of the Total Physical Response method are:

1. **acceleration of language acquisition:** Too much stress is the primary reason why many children do not stay with a foreign language. Total Physical Response is based on the premise that the child will speak fluently and with good pronunciation when he is ready, usually after 20 hours of consistent language exposure. If this process is forced the children may experience undue stress and will not speak spontaneously.
2. **long-term retention:** Dr. Asher has over 20 years of research to support his Total Physical Response theory that children and adults learn language at longer intervals if it is acquired naturally.
3. **good pronunciation:** Pronunciation is good because the children speak only after a long period of hearing the spoken language. Pronunciation will be near native particularly if the children begin their foreign language training before puberty.
4. **generates enthusiasm** for foreign language study. Enthusiasm results from a stress-free environment, a feeling of comradery among children and an element of surprise in the teaching.
5. is **compatible with Montessori school philosophy.** A Chinese proverb summarizes Total Physical Response, "When I hear, I forget. When I see, I remember. When I do, I learn."

The Total Physical Response method involves the use of commands by the parent or teacher. The child hears, understands and responds to the commands through a corresponding physical action. The right brain is subsequently tapped.

Please review the sample lesson below:

Recipe: Body Parts

Ingredients: Touch   the eyes
               Point to   the nose
                                the mouth

               Open   the eyes
               Close   the nose
                                the mouth

Recombination: Touch your eyes and close your mouth.

Variety: Close your nose and open your mouth.

Instructions:

1. Begin the lesson by saying to the children in English that you will be telling them to do something. They are to watch you as you do the activity and listen. They do not need to repeat the words. Simply listen and do.
2. The teacher then chooses two children to sit on either side of her. A sentence is modeled by the teacher. For example, "Touch your eyes." The children on either side follow suit by mimicking the teacher's actions.
3. The teacher continues, "Touch your nose." "Touch your mouth."
4. Several repetitions and demonstrations are made to ensure understanding and retention.
5. The teacher then chooses a child seated next to her and says, "John touch your eyes." If help is needed to refresh John's memory the teacher models the activity again.
6. Once the vocabulary has been demonstrated and internalized the teacher can call on other children in the class. "Timmy, touch your mouth." "Mary, open your eyes." "Martha, close your mouth," etc.
7. When the vocabulary has been internalized without hesitation by the children the teacher is ready to recombine sentences. An example might be: "John, close your nose and open your eyes." "Ted, touch Martha's nose and close her mouth."

Comments:

1. Since the TPR method uses the command form the tone of the teacher or parent is very important in the way the message is heard by the child. The use of commands by no means implies the use of coercion or dominance. Rather, gentle, supportive and confident direction is given the child to elicit an appropriate response.
2. Be precise in the demonstration. Do not accidentally scratch your head as you are presenting a lesson. The children will be confused and may mimic you.
3. Limit the lesson to 5 or 7 words at a time. In this instance, three new body parts and two actions were introduced. When the children have mastered two actions increase by two more actions. Do not introduce more than three new vocabulary items at a time. The activity then becomes an exercise in memorization and retention will be shorter.
4. Hesitation by the children indicates that they have not understood. Model the lesson again.

5. Speech is not required by the children. They are to simply watch and do. Some children will want to repeat the words. That is fine, but not necessary.
6. Once recombination of sentences begins the noise level will increase. The teacher is combining words in a zany and unpredictable way, i.e. "Put the banana in your nose and sneeze." The children are having fun. More importantly, they are acquiring language.

Tracy Terrell and Stephen Krashen in their book, **The Natural Approach,** outline the following principles of a natural language acquisition process. They are:

1. comprehension precedes production.
2. production emerges in stages.
3. goal is communication.
4. atmosphere is relaxed and non-stressful.

In a natural acquisition process the child acquires a second language in much the same way as his first language. The mother or caretaker simplified the language so that the child could understand. Language was tuned to the linguistic level of the child. Communication involved the here and now. It transmitted real messages.

James Asher takes the acquisition process one step further. He believes that language acquisition involves movement or physical response, a give and take, a reciprocity. The Total Physical Response method reproduces a child's early learning environment and by so doing provides a momentum for acquiring a language and retaining it over long periods of time. The focus is on what is said, not how it is said. Grammar accuracy comes much later, after hearing and using the language in action often.

The caretaker, bilingual parent or teacher, as the case may be, uses the target language regularly. The focus of communication is a topic which is interesting or meaningful to the child. The teacher or caretaker tries to help the child understand by modeling behavior and rephrasing.

Perhaps the most significant finding in the area of second language acquisition by children is that attitude is more important than aptitude. Some children are learners (left-brain orientation) of language but everyone is an acquirer. Young children need an atmosphere of low anxiety, motivation and self-confidence. This atmosphere can be created by allowing for a longer silent period. The children can listen and watch and are not required to speak too soon.

The Total Physical Response method allows the child to observe and absorb. Movement and manipulation of real objects engage the child's sense of wonder and mastery. The child is involved in a purposeful activity. The movement required in the activity activates the long-term retention process. Topics involving identification, i.e. (draw an "x" through no. 7), physical characteristics, i.e. (touch the biggest animal) and practical life situations, i.e. (get up, take off your pajamas, put on your clothes) create a meaningful environment for second language acquisition.

The rate and extent of language acquisition in young children will vary. Some children show a delay from one to six months for production. An important goal in the early stages of language acquisition is reducing stress. Stress is reduced in a safe, comfortable and relaxed environment. Stress is also reduced by a silent period and through acquisition activities. Acquisition activities involve new vocabulary through consistent exposure to the language, input that is understood, opportunities for the child to respond physically and/or orally and a sense of group belonging or cohesion. Specific acquisition activities will be presented in Chapter III.

Georgi Lozanov, a Bulgarian physician, psychiatrist and educational researcher, has spent more than twenty years investigating and applying the phenomenon of suggestion in a wide range of learning contexts. One important application is foreign language. Lozanov believes that suggestion operates as a constant communicative factor in all interchange. This suggestion operates primarily at the subconscious level. Suggestion can be a useful tool in helping children achieve more of their potential, particularly in foreign language.

A suggestive atmosphere would be an environment low in stress, high in rapport with the children and rich in interesting peripheral stimuli such as posters, charts, artifacts, etc. The teacher's attitude, enthusiasm, expertise and clothing each relay a powerful message to children.

A suggestive environment supports focusing on the whole situation or sentence rather than its parts. The parts may be examined incidentally but grammar, pronunciation and vocabulary are secondary to the main thrust of communicating an idea.

The study of suggestion is a whole-brain approach to second language acquisition. This means that both areas of the brain are tapped for maximum participation by the child. Soft music and role play enrich and enhance the child's ability to observe and absorb information.

Lozanov believes that significant psychological and physiological health benefits arise from tapping more of the child's potential through the art of suggestion.

We have discussed how essential attitude and a non-stressful environment are to acquiring a foreign language. Lozanov's suggestopedia (suggestion applied to education) says that if characteristics of joy, ease and rapid learning are not observed in children, chances are their brain reserves are not being tapped. While specific practical tips of suggestion will be outlined in Chapter IV some general observations can be discussed briefly now.

Lynn Dhority writes about the artful use of suggestion in foreign language teaching in his book, **Acquisition through Creative Teaching.** He states that the means of suggestion can be realized in the following ways:

1. through the presence of personality, poise, credibility in teacher; her trustworthiness.
2. by capitalizing on the playfulness, sense of wonder and excitement in children.
3. by ensuring that the presentation of materials is in harmony with a passive, highly receptive, relaxed state of mind in the children.
4. through factors exerting suggestive impact such as facial expression, voice intonation, pitch, rhythm, posture, etc.
5. by peripheral stimuli such as posters, charts, graphic illustration which remain in the long-term memory.

Dhority believes that the success of a lesson plan has at least as much to do with the rapport and atmosphere fostered with the children as with specific activities planned.

To summarize, we note that Krashen and Terrell propose a natural approach to language acquisition in which comprehension precedes production. James Asher's Total Physical Response method uses movement to assimilate language first through the body. Lozanov reveals the powerful impact of suggestion on the acquisition process. Each of the above principles and concepts are valuable contributions to the field of second language acquisition and can be applied at home or school.

CHAPTER III
Recipes for Success

When planning a foreign language curriculum for young children one must consider the following questions. How much time do I have with the children? What do I want to teach them in a given time frame? How do I go about teaching the material? How will I measure success? These questions will be addressed in five parts. They are time specifications, goals, content areas, recipes for success and evaluation.

Time Specifications

How much time do I have with the children is an important consideration in developing a foreign language program. Daily reinforcement of the language is the ideal. However, this may not be the norm. In my experience, the following time guidelines are effective with young children preferably in smaller groups.

Pre-school	10-15 minutes/per day
Kindergarten	15 minutes
Grades 1 and 2	20 minutes
Grades 3 and 4	25 minutes

I met with children in small groups of 6 or 8 twice a week and then met with large groups once a week. The small group time was used to review, introduce new material, to practice and to allow for more focused participation by the child. The large group time served to unite two or more levels of children, i.e. pre-school and kindergarten. The integrated setting provided modeling for the younger children and allowed the older children to teach. Large group activities such as song, dance, movement and rhythm activities promoted comradery among the children as well as additional reinforcement of material introduced in the small group setting. Space was available to me for large group activities and movement could occur more easily. The small group setting involved the use of puzzles, a chalkboard and manipulation of objects or pictures.

Keep in mind that three days a week of foreign language exposure is better than two, etc. Realize also that time constraints affect the goals of your program. Emphasis may need to be shifted from year to year.

Goals

The second consideration in planning a foreign language program is: What do I hope to accomplish in the time allotted? My experience revealed the following goals to be realistic and effective with small children.

1. Foreign language acquisition is an enjoyable experience.
2. Culture is introduced as an important part of foreign language instruction.
3. Communication is made possible through understanding language which is presented on a regular basis.
4. More materials are available by involving the children in the creation of same.

The first goal, making foreign language acquisition fun, is a natural progression of using Total Physical Response and a mixture of right and left brain activities. Children delight in repetition and rhythmic activities. They love to sing, draw, color and act. If the children know that the teacher will do anything she asks them to do, a level of trust evolves which sets the children at ease. If the children know they need not respond in the language until they are ready they will relax. Second language acquisition is enjoyable because it has evolved in an environment minimizing stress.

The second goal, cultural awareness, is introduced through pictures and/or tangible artifacts, objects, currency, clothing, food and music. Culture appeals to the child's five senses. Children can see the pictures or slides. They can feel the texture of the clothing and touch the currency. They can smell and taste the food. They can hear the music.

The third goal, communication, is an important element of foreign language acquisition. However, communicating in a foreign language is a process evolving over time. For some children communication is delayed anywhere from one to six months.

The first step towards communication is for the child to understand what the teacher is saying in the foreign language (listening comprehension). This understanding occurs through regular interaction with a foreign language speaker (comprehensible input). Once the child understands what is heard a simple yes or no or shrug of the shoulders serves as a communicative response. Some children will point. Others will touch. Still others will answer in English. Some will even help their friends. All of these responses involve communicating a message. The amount and sophistication of communication will depend on the age of the child, his attitude and cumulative interaction in the language. After longer exposure the child may say simple phrases, i.e. "Yes, I like it" or "It's red." Later the child may be able to say "Señora, What is a tiger?" This child has heard the teacher model the phrase, "What is a . . ." over and over again. Teacher input to the child can take the following form:

The tiger is an animal. The lion is an animal. But you are not an animal. The tiger is an animal. The tiger is big. Show me another animal that is big. The lion is big. Very good. The tiger is yellow. Is this yellow? The tiger is yellow. The tiger has eyes, nose and a mouth. You have eyes, nose and a mouth (pointing to them). The tiger has teeth. The tiger has ears. Look at his ears. His ears are small. Touch your ears. Let's review. The tiger is an animal. But we are not animals. The tiger is big. He is big like the lion. He is yellow not white. The tiger has eyes, nose and a mouth. The tiger has ears. His ears are small not big. His ears are small. Continuing . . . The tiger lives in the continent of Asia. Here is the continent of Asia. Put the tiger in the continent of Asia. Touch the tiger. Touch the continent of Asia. (Montessori children have reviewed continents earlier).

The above illustration indicates that it is highly recommended that the teacher speak in the foreign language as much as possible. The more language a child hears and understands from an adult the greater strides will be seen in foreign language acquisition. Movement and manipulation of physical objects, as outlined by the Total Physical Response method in Chapter II, will accelerate this acquisition process and promote long term retention of the second language.

The fourth goal, that of making materials, helps the children and teacher tremendously. The children can listen to directions in the foreign language and learn new vocabulary. They will understand color, number and location words. They will hear chunks of language and learn by doing. Making materials can be a Total Physical Response lesson for the children with results that will streamline the teacher's work.

Topics to Teach

Topics introduced to children in a foreign language should be of high interest to them. For example, very small children are fascinated by animals. They are also learning to color, to count and to make new friends. The program should be designed accordingly. As Maria Montessori once said, "Follow the child."

Foreign language instruction should be appropriate to the age level of the child. Older children can understand concepts like next to, between, over, under, etc. A 2-1/2 year old cannot. Remember, your goal as a teacher is to see the child succeed.

Some early elementary foreign language teachers like to write their programs to coincide with the skills being acquired by the children in the regular school curriculum (immersion). Montessori and/or pre-school teachers may incorporate material being presented in the classroom for that month in their program. I have found success having a time lapse for skills acquired in the regular classroom and those acquired in the foreign language program. Rather than teach a skill such as telling time simultaneously in the foreign language I prefer to see the child master the concept first in his native tongue. The child is increasing his knowledge of the world. He brings this knowledge to the second language which is recently being acquired. The transition is then made with ease. However, you can also successfully introduce a geography or social studies lesson prior to regular instruction in this area if it is meaningful and interesting to the child.

The number of topics presented in a year's time will depend on age level, attitude and time with the children. I have found that a variety of topics with a minimum of vocabulary for each topic works well in the beginning years. Vocabulary for these topics can be expanded year by year and increase in complexity. As the acquisition process evolves more topics can be added and the corresponding vocabulary finetuned.

The following list is a sample of topics which can be introduced in the pre-school and elementary school years.

1.	Identity	12.	Family
2.	Greetings	13.	Feelings
3.	Colors/Shapes	14.	House
4.	Numbers	15.	Classroom/Time
5.	Body Parts	16.	Calendar/Weather
6.	Physical Actions	17.	Seasons/Sports
7.	Directions	18.	Community
8.	Animals	19.	Professions
9.	Description	20.	Transportation
10.	Food	21.	Culture
11.	Clothing	22.	Holidays

EVALUATION

Success will be easily recognized using the Total Physical Response method with young children. If the children have understood what you have said they will be able to do the appropriate action or activity without hesitation.

If the child is eager to respond, whether he is guessing or not, you will know that the child is "tasting" language without fear or stress. In the early years, you can expect to see children using their newly acquired language by way of songs on the playground or by counting during fantasy play at home. After consistent exposure to a new language children will be able to answer simple questions using the known vocabulary they are acquiring. They will also be able to give simple descriptions of people or things.

A handy key to use for noting retention in children is the following:

O — knows response

Ø — hesitates but does correct thing

X — does not know

Pre-test of vocabulary items and physical actions are valuable at the beginning of the year to show the children how much they have remembered.

The best evaluation of course, is to let the children experience the thrill of understanding what the teacher is saying through consistent positive feedback. If you have a video camera the children can see their progress on film! If not, they can simply draw, pantomime, role-play, describe or follow instructions in the language.

Keep in mind that learning takes place during periods of high emotion. Present your topics in novel and interesting ways and the children will be delighted! Let's turn now to "recipes for success" as a critical component of a foreign language program for young children.

Recipes for Success

The following recipes have been organized by topic not by age level. The recipes can be grouped together to form a lesson or used independently depending on time constraints. For the most part, the 22 topic areas are presented sequentially with supporting activities and materials for acquisition. Prerequisite vocabulary is indicated as well as how to use particular vocabulary to create a recipe or lesson. The ideas and activities are in English. For your convenience, some recipes or lessons are translated into Spanish. However, these same recipes can be easily adapted to other languages.

Some recipes are simple. Some are more elaborate. No matter. They each satisfy children's "taste" for language. Some of the recipes have been authored. If you like what you read from a particular recipe feel free to contact that person for more information. Every "chef" enjoys positive feedback. Good Luck!

IDENTITY

MY NAME IS

Children enjoy using foreign names.
Make sure their new name is agreeable to them.
Explain the meaning of the * names.

Here are samples of Spanish names:

Muchachas

Adela	Carolina	Enriqueta	Inés	Margarita	Rebeca
Agustina	Catalina	Ernestina	Irene	María	Rita
Alberta	Cecilia	*Esperanza	Isabel	Marta	Rosa
Alicia	Celia	Ester	Josefina	Matildo	Sara
Amelia	Clara	*Estrella	Juana	Mercedes	Silvia
*Amanecer	Claudia	Eugenia	Judít	*Milagro	*Sol
Ana	*Concepción	Eva	Julia	Mónica	Solía
Andrea	Consuelo	Florencia	Laura	Noémi	Sonia
Ángela	*Corazón	Francisca	Leonor	Nora	Susana
Anita	Cristina	Genoveva	Lourdes	Norma	Teresa
Antonia	Diana	Georgina	Lucía	Olga	Valentina
Aurora	Dolores	Gertrudis	Luisa	Olivia	Verónica
Bárbara	Dorotea	Gisela	Lupe	Patricia	Victoria
Beatriz	Elena	Gloria	*Luz	Paula	*Violeta
Berta	Elisa	Graciela	Magdalena	Pilar	Virginia
Carlota	Emilia	Guadalupe	Manuela	Ramona	Yolanda
Carmen	Engracia	Hortensia	*Mañana	Raquel	

Muchachos

Abelardo	Cecilio	Felipe	Jaime	Mateo	Sansón
Agustín	César	Fernando	Javier	Mauricio	Santiago
Alano	Claudio	Fidel	Jerónimo	Miguel	Samuel
Alberto	Cristobal	Gerardo	Jesús	Nicolás	Saúl
Alejandro	Daniel	Gilberto	Joaquín	Oscar	Sebastian
Alfonso	David	Guido	Jorge	Pablo	Sergio
Alfredo	Diego	Guillermo	José	Patricio	Simón
Andrés	Domingo	Gustavo	Juan	Pedro	Terencio
Ángel	Donato	Hector	Julio	Rafael	Timoteo
Antonio	Edmundo	Hernando	Leonardo	Raimundo	Tomás
Armando	Eduardo	Horacio	Lorenzo	Ramón	Valentín
Arnaldo	Emilio	Huberto	Luís	Raúl	Vicente
Benito	Enrique	Hugo	Manuel	Ricardo	Victor
Benjamín	Ernesto	Humberto	Marcos	Roberto	Virgilio
Bernardo	Esteban	Ignacio	Mario	Rodolfo	
Carlos	Federico	Isidro	Martín	Rogelio	

Note: Foreign language names can be found in the back of the appropriate dictionary.

EL SOMBRERO

Nametags

Make sombrero nametags for name recognition to be worn around neck by
children during first few weeks of school.
Draw sombrero with 6-1/2" base and 4" height on yellow construction paper.
Print Spanish name in permanent magic marker.
Cover hat with clear contact paper.
Punch hole in top.
Thread through yarn 2' long and tie.

Envelopes

Store nametags in gold office envelopes.
The envelopes can be hung through the hole on hooks mounted on pegboard.
Each envelope corresponds to a distinct small group of children.
For example, small groups may be distinguished by color names or countries.
(Red, yellow, green, orange, white, blue or Perú, Chile, Argentina, Bolivia,
Ecuador).
When the "Perú" group is called those members go to the Spanish area of
classroom, select their name from the envelope, put it on and sit down.
This procedure works best in a pre-school setting or Montessori school.
After the first month of school the tags can be collected and returned at the end of
the year as souvenirs of Spanish class.

WHERE IS THUMBKIN?

Finger play using two puppets named Paco and Flaco.
Teacher demonstrates and sings first to Paco.
She puts puppet on one hand and sings.

Where is Paco? **(moving puppet, Paco up and down)**	¿Dónde está Paco?
Where is Paco? **(moving opposite index finger up and down)**	¿Dónde está Paco?
Here he comes. **(move puppet forward toward class)**	Ya viene.
Here he comes. **(move opposite index finger toward class)**	Ya viene.
Where is Paco? **(repeat actions for line 1)**	¿Dónde está Paco?
Where is Paco? **(repeat actions for line 2)**	¿Dónde está Paco?
There he goes. **(move puppet slowly out and around behind teacher's back)**	Ya se va.
There he goes. **(move opposite index finger in same direction)**	Ya se va.

Variation: Children's names may be substituted for Paco and Flaco.

One volunteer is seated in middle of class while class sings to child.

WHO IS IT?

Listening exercise and name recognition.
Children sit in large circle.
One child volunteers to sit in middle of circle with eyes closed.
Teacher selects one volunteer to shake maracas.
Child shakes maracas 3 times and places them quietly behind back.
Child in center of circle is instructed to open eyes.
Child tries to identify who shook the maracas.
Three guesses are permitted.

BALL ROLL

Children sit in a circle.
The teacher rolls the ball to a child and asks the question,
"Who is it?" or —¿Quién es?—
The child who receives the ball responds, "It is Mary" or —Es María—.
The child having the ball continues the game by rolling it to someone else and
  asking the original question.

TWO LITTLE GIRLS (OR BOYS)

Teacher has two child volunteers sit beside her.
Class chants to children.
When the child's name is called, he walks away from the teacher, then around the
  circle of seated children.
When the child's name is called again, he walks to the teacher and sits down.

Two little boys or (girls) sitting in a chair.	Dos muchachos sentando en la silla.
One named _____ .	Uno se llama _____ .
The other named _____ .	El otro se llama _____ .
Go away _____ .	Vaya _____ .
Go away _____ .	Vaya _____ .
Come back _____ .	Venga _____ .
Come back _____ .	Venga _____ .

SHOES

Children remove one shoe and place it in a box.
Teacher removes one shoe at a time from the box and asks, "Whose it it?" or
  —¿De quíen es?—
Class responds, "It is . . ." or —Es de . . .—

ROLL CALL

Teaches does roll call and asks, "Here?" —¿está?— or "Not here?" —¿no está?—.
Child responds, "here" —presente— or class responds "not here" —ausente—.

23

LONDON BRIDGES

Use this activity to reinforce the children's names.

London Bridges falling down,
    falling down,
    falling down,
London Bridges falling down,
(Two children slant hands upward to form bridge while others pass under.)
My fair lady.
(Child passing through is held back.)

Take the keys and lock her up,
    lock her up,
    lock her up,
Take the keys and lock her up,
(Child is tossed side to side.)
My fair lady.
(Child returns to stand behind bridge. Repeat.)

Sobre la puente marchan los niños
    marchan los niños
    marchan los niños
Sobre la puente marchan los niños

Pobrecita.

Ya tenemos _____ ,
    (name of child)
_____ ,
_____ ,
Ya tenemos _____ .

Pobrecita.

IDENTITY

Collect pictures from magazines of little boys and little girls.
Use as flashcards for class to identify.

SONG

(10 Little Indians tune)

What are you? (3X)
What are you? (3X)
What are you? (3X)
I am a boy or
I am a girl

¿Qué eres, qué eres, qué eres tú?
¿Qué eres, qué eres, qué eres tú?
¿Qué eres, qué eres, qué eres tú?
Yo soy un muchacho or
Yo soy una muchacha

Individual child responds, I am a girl or boy, as the case may be.

Game:

Children are standing in a circle.
They sing song as ball is being passed around the circle.
When the song is over whoever has the ball answers by saying whether he/she is a boy or a girl.
The child who responded then sits down and the game continues.

ACTIVITY

Child selects one of four flashcards, a man, woman, boy or girl (*hombre/mujer*).
Child holds it in front of face.
Class asks in unison, "What are you?" or —*¿Qué eres tú?*—
Child answers appropriately.

24

GREETINGS

PUPPETS

Teacher greets hand puppet by saying hello.   *¡Hola!*
Hand puppet greet teacher by saying hello.
Teacher then greets individual children by saying hello and shaking hands.
Repeat same for saying goodbye.   *¡Adiós!*

SONG
(Good Night Ladies tune)

Good-bye friends	*Adiós amigos*
Good-bye friends	*Adiós amigos*
Good-bye friends	*Adiós amigos*
God speed to you!	*¡Qué les vayan bien!*

GOOD DAY

Explain good morning, good afternoon and good night through picture cards.

Good morning   *Buenos días*
(rising sun, children eating breakfast)
Good afternoon   *Buenas tardes*
(full sun, children playing outside)
Good evening   *Buenas noches*
(moon, children sleeping)

ACTIVITY

Teacher indicates key word response and shows corresponding picture, i.e. Good
   Morning.
Teacher calls two children by name, i.e. *Ana y Tomás.*
They stand up, walk to the center of the circle, shake hands, greet each other and
   sit down.
New children continue to greet one another as teacher calls them by name.

START THE DAY

Good morning everybody,	*Buenos días clase.*
Good morning everybody,	*Buenos días clase.*
Good morning, (3X)	*Buenos días (3X)*
Smile everyone. Smile everyone.	*Sonrían todos. (2X)*
We'll shake the blues away.	*Ya el frío se fué.*
Shake hands everyone.	*Den las manos todos.*
Shake hands everyone.	*Den las manos todos.*
Let's make new friends today!	*¡Ya somos amigos today!*

SONG

(Happy Birthday tune)

Good morning to you,
Good morning to you,
Good morning, good morning,
Good morning to you.

Buenos días a ti,
Buenos días a ti,
Buenos días, buenos días,
Buenos días a ti.

HOW ARE YOU

Teacher chants. Class chants.

Hello class, how are you?
Fine thanks, teacher and how
'bout you?

Hola clase, ¿Cómo está?

Muy bien Señora y ¿Cómo le va?

SONG

Teacher selects volunteer to be the new friend for the day.
The class sings to that child.

Hello, how are you and how do
you do?
You'll feel right at home in a moment.
Hello. How are you?
We welcome our friend.
Hello. How are you?
Hello. How are you?
Hello. Hello. Hello.

¡Hola! ¿Cómo estás y cómo te vas?
Estarás cómodo en un momento.
¡Hola! ¿Cómo estás?
Saludamos a nuestro amigo.
¡Hola! ¿Cómo estás?
¡Hola! ¿Cómo estás?
¡Hola! ¡Hola! ¡Hola!

¡HOLA!

¡Ho - la! ¿Cómo estás y Có - mo te vas? Es -

ta - rás cómo - do en un momento ¡Ho - la! ¿Cómo estás?

Sa - lu - da - mos a nuestro a - migo. ¡Ho - la! ¿Cómo estás?

¡Ho - la! ¿Cómo estás? ¡Ho - la! ¡Ho - la! ¡Ho - la!

FRAY FELIPE

Fray Fe- li- pe Fray Fe- li- pe ¿Duer - mes

tú? ¿Duer- mes tú? To-ca la cam- pa- na,

To-ca la cam- pa- na, ¡Tan tan tan! ¡Tan tan tan!

Good morning. (2X)	*Buenos días. (2X)*
How are you? (2X)	*¿Cómo estás? ¿Cómo estás? (2X)*
Very fine, thanks. (2X)	*Muy bien, gracias. (2X)*
And yourself. (2X)	*Y usted. (2X)*
(Partners shake hands.)	
Good afternoon. (2X)	*Buenas tardes. (2X)*
Time to eat. (2X)	*A comer. (2X)*
Tortillas with cheese. (2X)	*Tortillas con el queso. (2X)*
How delicious they are!	*¡Qué ricas son! (2X)*
(Partners eat and rub tummies)	
Good night. (2X)	*Buenas noches. (2X)*
Time to sleep. (2X)	*A dormir. (2X)*
Give me a kiss. (2X)	*Dáme un beso. (2X)*
I love you. (2X)	*Te quiero. (2X)*
(Partners pretend to sleep and kiss.)	
Good-bye. (2X)	*Adiosito. (2X)*
Here I go. (2X)	*Ya me voy. (2X)*
See you tomorrow. (2X)	*Hasta mañana. (2X)*
God speed. (2X)	*Qué te vayas bien. (2X)*

DING-A-LING-A-LING

play telephones or toilet paper rolls

Introduce: **Hello**	**Good-bye**	**How are you? I am . . .**
Hola	*Adiós*	*¿Cómo estás? (good) Estoy bien.*
(phone) *Hablé*	*Hasta luego*	*¿Cómo te va? (bad) Estoy mal.*
Bueno	*Chau*	*(so -so) Así. Así.*
Diga		

Child chooses friend to call.

Juan: dials Miguel.
Miguel: answers *(Hablé, Bueno, etc.)*
Juan: *Hola, Miguel, Es Juan.*
Miguel: *Hola, Juan. ¿Cómo te va?*

Juan: *Estoy . . . (bien, mal or así así)*
Miguel: *Estoy . . . (bien, mal or así así)*
Juan: *Adiós, Miguel.*
Miguel: *Adiós, Juan.*

COLORS

red	*rojo*
blue	*azul*
yellow	*amarillo*
orange	*anaranjado*
white	*blanco*
black	*negro*
brown	*pardo*
purple	*violeta*
green	*verde*
pink	*rosado*
grey	*gris*

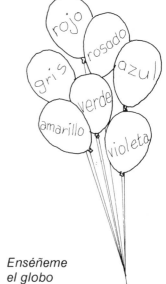

BAG OF BALLOONS

balloons	Show me	*Enséñeme*
bag	the balloon	*el globo*

A bag of balloons is placed in the center of the circle.
One child volunteers to find the balloon which the teacher has requested.
The child then gives the teacher the appropriate colored balloon and sits down.

COLOR WHEEL

white mat board 12" x 16"
crayons
1 metal fastener
1 manilla strip

Draw a large circle in the center of the mat board.
Divide the circle into 11 parts of a pie.
Color each part a different color.
Punch hole in the center of the circle using scissor tip.
Make one manilla strip 1/2" x 2-1/2"
Punch hole in strip not too close to edge.
Insert fastener.

Teacher spins
Children identify color.

MONTESSORI 3-PERIOD LESSON

Introduce three colors at a time.

Point to	*Apunte a*
Touch	*Toque*
Pass me	*Páseme*

1. This is red. This is yellow. This is blue.
2. Where is red? Where is yellow? Where is blue?
3. What is this?

GO FISH

Cards   *Los Naipes*
  tag board
  crayons
  scissors
  Avery colored dots
  contact paper

Draw an oval fish approximately 3″ wide by 5″ long.
Include a small fin having triangular shape at ends.
Have children color each fish a different color.
Apply one Avery dot for the eye.
Contact fish and cut out.

Game
Depending on size of group each child receives from 3-5 cards.
Remaining cards go in the "Go Fish" pile.
Child asks neighbor, "Do you have red?," or —¿*Tienes rojo?*—
If neighbor does not have red the first child must select a card from the "Go
  Fish" pile.
The object is to pair up matches.
Winner has most matches.

Variation
Teacher deals 3-5 cards to each child.
Teacher asks, "Who has yellow?" or —¿*Quién tiene amarillo?*—
All those having yellow put their yellow in the center of the circle.
Teacher continues until all the colors have been accounted for.
This is a good recipe for reinforcing color names for children who have not yet
  mastered them.

MARBLES

marbles   *juego de canicas*
brown bag

This activity is a variation of the Go Fish game.
Teacher passes out 5 marbles to each child.
Child hides marbles in lap.
The remaining marbles are placed in a brown bag.
First child asks neighbor, "Do you have red?"
Child is looking for matches.   *hace juego*
If a match is not found the child must take a marble out of the brown bag.
Winner has most matches.

HOT POTATO

small brown lunch bag
colored fish cards

Children sit in a circle.
Teacher shakes a tambourine while children pass bag to one another.
When tambourine stops whoever has the bag reaches in, chooses a color and
  identifies it.

LIGHT OR DARK?

Claro o oscuro

Use Montessori color tablets to illustrate distinction.

SONG

(Are You Sleeping tune)

construction paper

Children are given large colored piece of construction paper.
As their color is sung they go to the front of the room and take a bow.

The colors, the colors	*Los colores, los colores*
What are they	*¿Cuáles son?*
Red, red	*Rojo, rojo*
Very good, very good	*Muy bien, muy bien.*

LOS COLORES

Los co- lo- res   Los co- lo- res   ¿Cuál- es

son?   ¿Cuál- es   son?   Trái- ga me el   ro- jo

Trái ga me el   ro- jo   muy bi- en   muy bi - en

I KNOW

Yo sé mis colores

Teacher says: "I know my colors" and then says a color.
Next child repeats statement, says first color and adds another.
Activity continues until someone cannot remember all the colors.

COLOR FANS

Los abanicos

8-1/2" x 11" white paper
crayons

Fold the paper like this.	*Doblen el papel así.*
First forward and then back.	*Primero, adelante y después, atrás*
Forward and back. (3X)	*Adelante y atrás. (tres veces)*
Now we have a fan.	*Ahora tenemos un abanico.*
Color the first part red.	*Coloren la primera parte roja.*
Next yellow.	*Después amarilla.*
Next blue, etc.	*Después azul, etc.*
How pretty the fan is!	*¡Qué lindo es el abanico!*

BINGO

white paper 8-1/2" x 11"	el papel
pencils	el lápiz
rulers	la regla
crayons	los creyones
pennies	los centavos

Boards

Put the paper like this.	Pongan el papel así.
Take your pencil and draw 4 lines from top to bottom.	Tomen sus lapices y dibujen cuatro líneas de arriba abajo.
Like this.	Así.
Now draw three lines across the paper. Like this.	Ahora dibujen tres lineas a través del papel. Así.
In the center of the paper draw an "X." Like this.	En el centro del papel dibujen una equis. Así.
Color each square a different color. Like this.	Pinten cada cuadrado un color distinto. Así.

Game

Teacher calls a color.
Children cover the color with a marker.
First child to cover a line either down, across or diagonally wins.

1, 2, 3 What color is it?   Uno, dos, tres ¿Qué color es?

strands of colored yarn (little girls use in hair) or feathers from notions in dimestore.

Teacher places strands of yarn behind back.
Teacher pulls out one strand, holds it up and says, "What color is it?"

1, 2, 3 Look and See   Uno, dos, tres, Miren y Vean

squares of different colors

Teacher places three colors in a row.
Children look at colors.
Children close their eyes.
Teacher takes away one color.
Children open their eyes.
Children guess which color is missing.   ¿Qué falta?

BOOKS AND GAMES

Read story **Little Blue and Little Yellow** by Leo Leonni.

Play **The Old Shoe Game** by Selchow & Righter Company or **Girocolor** by Discovery Toys.

WATERCOLORS

Experiment with mixing colors.

Red and blue makes purple.
Blue and yellow makes green.
Orange and blue makes brown.

PINWHEELS

white paper cut 5" square
straight pins
pencils
crayons

Take your pencil and make a point in the middle of the paper. Like this.	*Tomen el lápiz y hagan un punto en el medio del papel. Así.*
Draw two lines diagonally. One like this. The other like this.	*Dibujen dos líneas diagonalmente. Una así. La otra así.*
Color each part or triangle a different color. Like this.	*Coloren cada parte o triángulo un color distinto. Así.*
Now cut the lines up to the point. Do not cut the point.	*Ahora, corten las lineas hasta el punto. No corten el punto.*
Take the first part and fold it in. Skip the next part.	*Tomen la primera parte y dóblenla adentro. No hagan esta parte.*
Take the next part and fold it in. Skip the next part.	*Tomen la siguiente y dóblenla así. No hagan esta parte.*
Take the next part and fold it in. Skip the next part.	*Tomen la siguiente y dóblenla así. No hagan esta parte.*
Take the last part and fold it in.	*Tomen la siguiente y dóblenla.*
Pick up the pin. Push the pin into the eraser of the pencil. Like this.	*Tomen el alfiler. Empujen el alfiler en la goma del lápiz. Así.*
Very good. Now blow!	*Muy bien. ¡Ahora soplen!*

FRUIT LOOP BRACELETS

Fruit Loop cereal
thin wire

Each small group of children has bowl of cereal filled with fruit loops.
Teacher instructs children which colors to place on necklace.
When finished, children **twist** wire and have a bracelet to wear.

Take the wire.	*Tomen la cuerda metálica.*
Measure 8 inches.	*Midan ocho pulgadas de largo.*
Cut the wire.	*Corten la cuerda metálica.*
Put on . . . red, etc.	*Pongan rojo, etc.*
Twist the wire.	*Tuerzan la cuerda metálica.*
Now you have a bracelet.	*Ahora, tienen una pulsera.*

DOT-TO-DOT

ditto of each of the shapes
pencils

Children connect dots and identify shape.

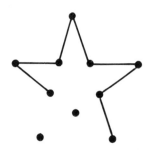

COLORS AND SHAPES

circle	*el círculo*
square	*el cuadrado*
rectangle	*el rectángulo*
star	*la estrella*
diamond	*el diamante*
oval	*el óvalo*

red, blue, and yellow construction paper.

Teacher prepares 15-20 triangles, circles, rectangles, stars, etc., in various colors.
The colored shapes are laid out in front of the children.
The teacher instructs one child to pass her any of the following:

    2 blue circles
    2 red triangles
    1 yellow star and 1 red rectangle
    3 blue squares, etc.

STAND UP TWISTER

large felt pieces 12" square.

This activity is a variation of the American Twister game.
It reviews six shapes.

Teacher cuts out triangles, circles, stars, rectangles, etc. from colored felt.
The shapes are glued onto white felt squares.
Several squares of the same shape and color can be made.
Teacher asks children to find the following shapes.
The children scramble to stand on the nearest appropriate shape and color.

Find a yellow triangle.	*Encuentren un triángulo amarillo.*
Find a blue circle.	*Encuentren un círculo azul.*
Find a red star.	*Encuentren una estrella roja.*
Find a green diamond.	*Encuentren un diamante verde.*
Find a black rectangle.	*Encuentren un rectángulo negro.*
Find a orange square.	*Encuentren un cuadrado anaranjado.*
Find a purple oval.	*Encuentren un óvalo violeto.*

WHAT WILL IT BE?

white paper
crayons

Teacher cuts out a shape anywhere on a 8-1/2" x 11" piece of white paper.
She repeats process for all papers.
Children receive papers and must draw something using the cut out shape as part
    of their picture.
Later class discusses what was drawn.

Variation: Children draw pictures using as many shapes as they can. Later they
    discuss what shapes were used and what colors they are.

PICK UP STICKS   *Palitos*

Use pick up sticks to make a triangle, a star, a diamond, a square, or rectangle.
Teacher directs child: Take 1 red stick, 1 yellow stick and 1 blue stick.
Make a triangle.   *Haga un triángulo.*

NUMBERS

Units	Tens	Hundreds	Thousands
uno	*diez*	*ciento*	*mil*
dos	*veinte*	*doscientos*	*dos mil*
tres	*treinta*	*trescientos*	*tres mil*
cuatro	*cuarenta*	*cuatrocientos*	*cuatro mil*
cinco	*cincuenta*	*quinientos*	*cinco mil*
seis	*seiscenta*	*seiscientos*	*seis mil*
siete	*setenta*	*setecientos*	*siete mil*
ocho	*ochenta*	*ochocientos*	*ocho mil*
nueve	*noventa*	*novecientos*	*nueve mil*
diez	*cien*	*mil*	*diez mil*

10 LITTLE INDIANS

Activity
Children are given number flashcards.
They sing 10 Little Indians.
When their number is called they go to front of room and take a bow.

Song
One little, two little, three little Indians	*Uno, dos, tres inditos*
four little, five little, six little Indians	*cuatro, cinco, seis inditos*
seven little, eight little, nine little Indians	*siete, ocho, nueve inditos*
ten little Indian boys and girls.	*diez inditos son.*

Variation
little dogs, little kittens, little children   *perritos, gatitos, niñitos*

UNO

pack of Uno cards
chalkboard ledge

Uno cards include the colors yellow, blue, green, and red.
They are numbered from 1-9.
This is an interesting activity for young children and reviews number and color recognition.

Teacher places about 15 Uno cards on chalkboard ledge.
Teacher directs children to do the following:

Bring me the yellow two.	*Tráigame el dos amarillo.*
Show me the red three.	*Enséñeme el tres rojo.*
Show me the green five.	*Enséñeme el cinco verde.*
Bring me three blue two's.	*Tráigame tres tarjetas del número dos y de color azul.*

BINGO

Standard Bingo game can be played to review alphabet and numbers 1-100.

Variation:
Bingo numbers can be placed in a container.
Child then chooses a chip and identifies the number.

ROCKET SHIP

Ferndale Elementary Schools
Ferndale, Michigan

Reviews numbers 1-10.

Children are in a circle.

They squat standing on floor with one hand raised like tip of rocket over their heads.

Children begin counting from 1 up to 10 raising their bodies slowly as they approach 10.

When 10 is called out they all blast off.

After blast off they can then begin counting again from one to ten crouching down as they go.

Upon reaching 10 the children should all be sitting back down in their original space.

Children love this activity.

Some children will want to blast off early or crash early.

Be sure that the game stops and those children remain seated before continuing.

DICE

2 large styrofoam dice (available from some school products warehouses)

Children are seated in a circle.

Teacher selects a volunteer to toss one dice (for lower numbers 1-6).

Child identifies number which lands face up.

Later, two dice can be thrown at a time and the numbers rearranged to include all possibilities such as 12 or 21.

EXERCISE

faster	*más rápido*
slower	*más despacio*

Children are seated in a circle with feet outstretched in front of them.

They sing:

and 1 and 2	*y uno y dos*
and 3 and 4	*y tres y cuatro*
and 5 and 6	*y cinco y seis*
and 7 and 8	*y siete y ocho*

while raising first one leg and then the other.

Teacher can then say, "Now, faster or now slower."

The class moves legs accordingly as they count.

DOT-TO-DOT

Teacher draws a simple picture of an object, animal, place, or person.

The dots on the picture are each numbered.

However, the numbers are not in sequence.

The teacher calls out the numbers (i.e. 1-20-4-8-10), etc. and children connect the dots accordingly.

Variation:

Teacher draws simple sketch of a noun using 10 or 12 dots.

Each dot has the number word next to it instead of the number.

Children connect the dots by reading number words from one to twelve.

They discover what the noun is and learn a new word.

MOTHER MAY I?

step	*un paso*
small	*pequeño*
medium	*mediano*
big	*grande*
Mother may I?	*¿Mamá, me das permiso?*
Yes, go ahead	*Sí, adelante*

Children are standing in a line across the room.

Teacher is facing them but at opposite end of the room.

The teacher commands one child at a time to take a number of small, medium or big steps.

Before moving, the child must remember to say, **Mother May I?**

If the child does not remember, he stays behind and the next child is called.

A **small** step is taken by placing one foot at the tip of the other and moving forward a determined number of steps.

A **medium** step is taken by casually walking one step at a time.

A **large** step is taken by stretching one foot as far in front of the other as is possible and proceeding.

Whoever touches the teacher first wins the game.

If a child forgets to ask permission in the middle of the game he must go back to the starting lineup.

Sequence

Tom, you may take four medium steps.	*Tomás, puedes tomar cuatro pasos medianos.*
Mother may I?	*¿Mamá, me das permiso?*
Tom takes four medium steps.	*Sí, adelante.*

BALL BOUNCE   *Rebote la pelota*

Children are seated in a circle.

First, the teacher demonstrates how to bounce the ball.

Teacher chooses one volunteer to stand in the middle of the circle and bounce the ball.

Child bounces the ball from one to ten times.

The class identifies the number of bounces.

*Young children from 2 -1/2 to 4 may have difficulty with this maneuver.

BALL PASS

Children pass a ball around and count out loud in sequence.

Note:

Children love passing things.

However, in their enthusiasm they may get carried away and begin throwing the ball.

Show them how to pass the ball slowly, using both hands.

FLOWER GARDENS

Jardín de flores

Myriam Met
First Start in Spanish
National Textbook Co.

construction paper
color tissue paper cut in to 2" squares
glue

Children twist once and glue colored tissue squares onto paper.
They describe their garden:

I have 6 flowers.	*Tengo 6 flores.*
One is red.	*Una es roja.*
Two are blue.	*Dos son azules.*
Three are yellow.	*Tres son amarillas.*

"DICE" WORK

dice
chalk

Pick up the dice.	*Tome los dados.*
Throw the dice.	*Tire los dados.*
How many are there?	*¿Cuántos hay?*
Pick up the chalk.	*Tome la tiza.*
Write the number on the board.	*Escriba el número en la pizarra.*
Draw a circle around the number.	*Dibuje un círculo alrededor del número.*

Repeat procedure.
Draw a triangle, square, etc. around the number.

AQUARIUM

El acuario

shapes vocabulary
white paper
crayons
pictures of fish

Draw a large rectangle.	*Dibujen un rectángulo grande.*
Draw some water. Like this.	*Dibujen el agua. Así.*
Now draw some fish.	*Ahora dibujen los peces.*
Color the fish.	*Coloren los peces.*
How many fish are there?	*¿Cuántos peces hay?*
Count them.	*Cuenten los peces.*

CLAP 8

Pálmese ocho

Teacher selects child volunteer to clap certain number of times.

MEXICAN NURSERY RHYME

4, 5, 6 cho—	*cuatro, cinco, seis, cho—*
4, 5, 6 co—	*cuatro, cinco, seis, cho—*
4, 5, 6 la—	*cuatro, cinco, seis, la—*
4, 5, 6 te—	*cuatro, cinco, seis, te—*
Chocolate, chocolate	*Chocolate, chocolate*
Beat, beat the chocolate	*Bate, bate el chocolate*

ADD OR SUBTRACT?

11	once	16	dieciséis
12	doce	17	diecisiete
13	trece	18	dieciocho
14	catorce	19	diecinueve
15	quince	20	veinte

5 plus 8 = 13
15 minus 6 = 9

5 más 8 son 13
15 menos 6 son 9

BEFORE/AFTER

antes/después

clothesline
number flashcards
clothespins

Teacher pins flashcards to clothesline.
She explains concept of before and after by pointing to cards coming before or after a particular number.

What number comes before 2?

¿Qué numero viene antes del número 2?

What number comes after 8?

¿Qué numero viene después del número 8?

What number comes after 5?

¿Qué numero viene después del número 5?

What number comes before 4?

¿Qué numero viene antes del número 4?

THE BALL

La Pelota

3 balls of various sizes

A little ball.
A bigger ball.
A great big ball I see.
Can you count them.
1 2 3.

Una pelota pequeña.
Una pelota grande.
La pelota más grande.
Cuenten las pelotas.
Uno-dos-tres.

CAKE

La Torta

picture of cake
box of candles
paper
crayons

Draw a cake.
How old are you?
Good. Draw _____ candles.
Count the candles.
How many candles are there?

Dibujen una torta.
¿Cuántos años tiene?
Bien. Dibujen _____ velitas.
Cuenten las velitas.
¿Cuántas velitas hay?

Teacher goes around group reviewing how old each child is.

WHICH IS WHICH?

Teacher holds up two number flashcards and asks, "Which is bigger or which is smaller?"

Cards may also be laid on the floor for the class to determine which is the biggest or smallest number.

Which is bigger?	¿Cuál es más grande?
Which is smaller?	¿Cuál es más pequeño?
Which is the biggest number?	¿Cuál es el número más grande?
Which is the smallest number?	¿Cuál es el número más pequeño?

CHANT

uno, dos, tres . . . los lápices
cuatro, cinco, seis . . . Enero es un mes.
siete, ocho, nueve . . . Ahora llueve.

NUMBER CARDS

3 x 5 index cards
magic markers

Make a set of cards as illustrated below.
Be sure each place value is in a different color.

1	10	100
2	20	200
3	30	300

The child is asked for the number 21.
He then selects the 20 card and the 1 card.

NUMBER LINE

one large white posterboard approximately 3-1/2' x 2' wide
crayola magic markers
crayons
pencil
ruler
plastic marker discs

Write the numbers from 1-100, ten at a time, across the poster board.
Each ten numbers should be written in a different color.

Example: red — 1, 2, 3, 4, 5, 6, 7, 8, 9, 10
blue — 11, 12, 13, 14, 15, 16, 17, 18, 19, 20
Child is asked to read the red line, for example, or:
Teacher selects child volunteer.
Volunteer takes a plastic disc, stands and closes eyes.
The child then tosses the disc.
The child opens eyes and identifies what number the disc is on.

SONG

(Are You Sleeping tune)

Children are given number flashcard.
As their number is sung, they go to the front of the room and take a bow.

The numbers, the numbers	Los números, los números
What are they? (2X)	¿Cuáles son? (2X)
Bring me number five,	Tráigame el cinco
Very good, very good.	Muy bien, muy bien.

BUZ

Maggie D'Allemand
Detroit Country Day School
Bloomfield Hills, Michigan

Children can be seated at desks or standing around the room.
Teacher gives a number such as 5.
Children begin counting.
When they arrive at 5, a multiple of 5, or a number containing the number 5, they
say, "Buzz" and go on to the next number.

Example:
1-2-3-4-buzz-6-7-8-9-buzz-11-12-13-14-buzz-16-17-18-19-buzz
50's would all be buzz.

NUMBER, SHAPE BOOK

black construction paper 8-1/2" x 5-1/2"
white paper
multicolored shapes precut by teacher
glue
pencils

The first page of the book is made of black construction paper.
Child makes addition problem by gluing shapes in sequence.
    i.e. 3 orange squares and 3 blue diamonds
The second page of the book is of white paper.
Child writes number problem which has been illustrated on the page before.
    i.e. 3 + 3 = 6

Children add as many pages as they wish.
Later they read their books to the teacher, i.e.

Page 1 — I have three orange squares and 3 blue diamonds.
Page 2 — 3 plus 3 equals 6.

$$\square\ \square\ \square + \Delta\ \Delta\ \Delta =$$
$$3\ +\ 3\ =\ 6$$

40

NUMBER WHEEL

Rueda de Números

paper
pencils

Draw a small circle. Like this.	*Dibujen un círculo pequeño. Así.*
Write the number 12 inside	*Escriban número doce dentro*
the circle.	*del círculo.*
Draw a bigger circle.	*Dibujen un círculo grande*
around the number 12.	*alrededor del número doce.*
Now draw the biggest circle	*Ahora dibujen el círculo más grande*
around the other circles.	*alrededor de los otros círculos.*
Like this.	*Así.*
Draw 6 lines through the circles.	*Dibujen seis líneas por los círculos.*
Like this.	*Así.*
Write number 4 and number	*Escriban número cuatro y número*
8 in these two parts. Look.	*ocho en éstas dos partes. Miren.*
Number 4 plus number 8 equals	*Cuatro más ocho son doce.*
number 12.	
What other numbers make 12?	*¿Qué otros números hacen doce?*

READ

Anno's Counting Book, by Mitsumasa Anno, Philomel Books (Putnam Publishing),
New York.

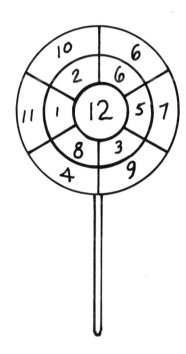

BODY PARTS

Las partes del cuerpo

face	*la cara*
eyes	*los ojos*
nose	*la nariz*
mouth	*la boca*
teeth	*los dientes*
ears	*las orejas*
head	*la cabeza*
neck	*el cuello*
chest	*el pecho*
stomach	*el estómago*
foot	*el pie*
leg	*la pierna*
hand	*la mano*
fingers	*los dedos*
arm	*el brazo*
knee	*la rodilla*
hair	*el pelo*
shoulders	*los hombros* (shrug shoulders)
lips	*los labios*
tongue	*la lengua*

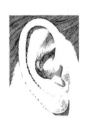

BODY BEAUTIFUL

white butcher paper that comes on a roll 36″ wide
pencils
crayons
hat
body part pictures

Children trace life-size body of another child.
Each child then selects a piece of paper having a body part on it from a hat.
Child says the body part and draws it on the body.

POTATOES OR PUZZLES?

Mr. Potato Head	*Señor Patata*
puzzles of clown face or animal body parts	*rompecabezas*
Take out the eyes.	*Saque los ojos.*
Take out the mouth.	*Saque la boca.*
Put in the mouth.	*Meta la boca.*

PEPE

Ramiro Garcia
Prospect High School
Saratoga, California

one Halloween skeleton

Touch	Toque
Point to	Apunte a
Take	Tome
Put	Ponga
Scratch	Rasque
skeleton	el esqueleto
body	el cuerpo

This is a skeleton.	Este es un esqueleto.
His name is Pepe.	Se llama Pepe.
Pepe has a body.	Pepe tiene un cuerpo.
The body has parts like you and me.	El cuerpo tiene partes como nosotros.

Touch Pepe's eyes.	Toque los ojos de Pepe.
Touch Pepe's mouth.	Toque la boca de Pepe.
Touch Pepe's foot.	Toque el pie de Pepe.

Point to Pepe's stomach.	Apunte al estómago de Pepe.
Point to Pepe's head.	Apunte a la cabeza de Pepe.
Point to Pepe's hand.	Apunte a la mano de Pepe.

Scratch Pepe's nose.	Rasque la nariz de Pepe.
Scratch Pepe's ear.	Rasque la oreja de Pepe.
Scratch Pepe's head.	Rasque la cabeza de Pepe.

Take Pepe's hand and scratch his stomach.	Tome la mano de Pepe y rasque el estómago.
Take Pepe's foot and put it in his mouth.	Tome el pie de Pepe y póngalo en la boca.
Take Pepe's right hand and put it on his foot.	Tome la mano derecha de Pepe y póngala en el pie.

BALLOONS FOR SALE

balloons of various colors
magic markers

Draw	Dibuje
smile	la sonrisa

Teacher directs children to draw particular facial features on the balloon one at a time.

Teacher can then print child's Spanish name on balloon.

The balloons can be tied to hook in coat room for take home.

SIMON SAYS

Teacher is Simon.

She prefaces commands by saying, **Simon says** . . . "Touch your eyes."

If teachers does not say **Simon says,** and child touches body part anyway the child must sit down.

Last child standing wins.

Simons says, touch your mouth!	Simón dice, ¡Tóquense la boca!
Simons says, touch your teeth!	Simón dice, ¡Tóquense los dientes!
Simons says, touch your nose!	Simón dice, ¡Tóquense la nariz!

WHEEL OF FORTUNE

See Color Wheel for construction.

Note:

Wheel is designed for small group use.
If used in larger group the wheel will need to be made accordingly.

Body parts are drawn on pie pieces of wheel.
Magic marker shows up best for large group use.
The wheel can be placed on an easel.
Child spins the wheel.
When the wheel stops the child names the body part.
Team naming most parts wins.

GO FISH

See Go Fish under "Colors" for game rules.

cards
tag board
scissors
glue
magazine pictures of human or animal body parts
contact paper

Children love this game.
They are particularly fascinated with seeing animal body parts such as donkey ears, elephant ears and rabbit ears on the cards.
National Geographic magazines usually contain a wealth of animal pictures.

DOCTOR'S OFFICE

Puffed Wheat cereal for pills	*las píldoras*
pencil	
paper	
plastic syringe	*la inyección*
medicine bottle	*la medicina*
plastic stethoscope	*el estetoscopio*
patient	*el paciente*

Teacher is doctor.
Doctor asks name, age and what hurts child.
Doctor prescribes medicine, shot, rest in bed, etc.

What is your name?	*¿Cómo se llama usted?*
How old are you?	*¿Cuántos años tiene usted?*
What hurts you?	*¿Qué le duele?*

My head hurts.	*Me duele la cabeza.*
My stomach hurts.	*Me duele el estómago.*
My foot hurts.	*Me duele el pie.*

You need a pill, a shot, medicine or rest.	*Necesita una píldora, una inyección, medicina o descanso.*

SONG

body part picture cards

Pass the hand to the right	*Pasa la mano a la derecha*
to the right	*a la derecha*
to the right	*a la derecha*
Whoever has the hand	*Quien tiene la mano*
Hooray! Hooray!	*¡Bravo! ¡Bravo!*
Now you touch your hand.	*Ya tocas la mano.*

Pass the body part to the left.
Substitute other body parts.

SONG

Poor little one	*Pobrecito*
What is wrong?	*¿Qué te pasa?*
Why oh why	*¿Por qué por qué*
Are you at home?	*Estás en casa?*
Ow, ow my head hurts.	*Me duele mucho la cabeza.*
Ow, ow his head hurts.	*Le duele mucho la cabeza.*

POBRECITO

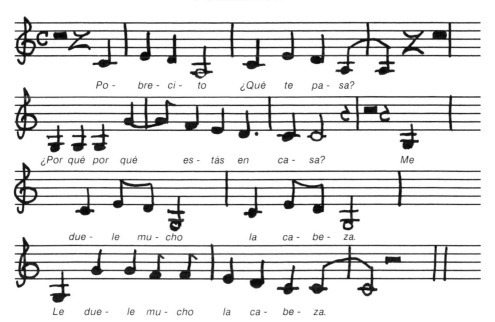

45

BODY TWIST

Touch your nose with your finger.
Touch your foot with your mouth.
Touch your leg with your arm.
Touch your ears with your hands.
Touch your eyes with your knees.
Touch your knee with your nose.
Touch your shoulder with your ear.
Touch your fingers with your fingers.
Touch your leg with your foot.
Touch your head with your knees.

Tóquense la nariz **con** el dedo.
Tóquense el pie **con** la boca.
Tóquense la pierna **con** el brazo.
Tóquense las orejas **con** las manos.
Tóquense los ojos **con** las rodillas.
Tóquense la rodilla **con** la nariz.
Tóquense el hombro **con** la oreja.
Tóquense los dedos **con** los dedos.
Tóquense la pierna **con** el pie.
Tóquense la cabeza **con** las rodillas.

Variation:

Can your touch your foot with your mouth? Yes/No. I can't.

¿Pueden tocar el pie con la boca?
Si/No. No, puedo.

SONG
(This Is The Way I Wash tune)

This is the way I wash my nose,
    wash my nose,
    wash my nose,
This is the way I wash my nose,
So early in the morning.

Substitute other body parts.

Así me lavo la nariz,
    la nariz,
    la nariz,
Así me lavo la nariz,
Cada mañana.

LINGO

Bingo cards (See "colors")
pennies, pebbles or plastic markers

Make up bingo cards of body parts.
Teacher calls out body part.
Child covers picture with marker.
First child to cover all parts in a row across, down, or diagonally wins.

SONG
(All Around The Mulburry Bush tune)

Ferndale Elementary Schools
Ferndale, Michigan

Teacher and children touch eyes, nose, and mouth as they sing.
On the Line, "We're all going to clap," everyone turns around and claps as they are
    turning.

Eyes, nose, and mouth (3X)
We're all going to clap

Ojos, nariz y boca (3X)
Vamos a aplaudir.

Hair, eyes, and teeth (3X)
We're all going to clap

Pelo, orejas y dientes (3X)
Vamos a aplaudir.

Hands, arms, and legs (3X)
We're all going to clap

Manos, brazos y piernas (3X)
Vamos a aplaudir.

HAIR

Use miniature plastic pop-off doll heads and place on fingertips.
Teacher greets each hair color and says good-bye.

COLOR THE HAIR

crayons
ditto

Teacher passes out ditto of three circles.
A hair color is written under each circle.
Child colors appropriate hair color as dictated by teacher.
Children may also draw in the eyes, nose, mouth, ears, etc.

blond hair	*pelo rubio*
brown hair	*pelo castaño*
black hair	*pelo negro*

CONCENTRATION

Teacher instructs children to close their eyes.
Teacher then places six body parts face up on floor.
Each body part is covered with a color.
  (Color and body part squares are same size.)
Children open eyes.
First volunteer names color and body part underneath.
Can be played like tic-tac-toe with more cards or simply as identification game.

COLOR THE PARTS

ditto of person
crayons

Color the eyes blue.	*Pinten los ojos azules.*
Color the nose red.	*Pinten la nariz roja.*
Color the ears pink.	*Pinten las orejas rosadas.*
Color the hair brown.	*Pinten el pelo pardo.*
Color the mouth purple.	*Pinten la boca violeta.*
Color the arms yellow.	*Pinten los brazos amarillos.*
Color the legs black.	*Pinten las piernas negras.*
Color the hands orange.	*Pinten las manos anaranjadas.*
Color the feet grey.	*Pinten los pies grises.*
Color the stomach green.	*Pinten el estómago verde.*

EL MONSTRUO

Teacher dictation.
Draw a monster having three eyes, a big nose, one leg, two stomachs, etc.

THINKING CAP

Teacher models "thinking" and illustrates "begin with" on board.

I am thinking of a body part that begins with: *Estoy pensando en una parte del cuerpo que empieza con:*

    b — *la boca, el brazo*
    c — *la cabeza, la cara, el cuerpo*
    d — *los dientes, los dedos*
    e — *el estómago*
    h — *los hombros*
    l — *los labios*
    m — *la mano*
    n — *la nariz*
    o — *los ojos, las orejas*
    p — *el pelo, el pie, el pierna, el pecho*
    r — *la rodilla*

IDENTIFICATION BY NUMBERS

ditto of person

Teacher passes out body part picture.
Each part is numbered.
Teacher asks, "What is number 1?"
Child identifies body part marked no. 1.

Variation:
Body part names are typed in corner of ditto.
Children label body parts by using word key on ditto.
Can also be cut and paste activity in which the children paste the words onto the body parts.

CHALKBOARD

body parts
shapes

Teacher draws isolated body parts all over the chalkboard.
Child is instructed to do the following:

Draw a circle around the mouth.   *Dibuje un círculo alrededor de la boca.*

Draw a square around the ear.   *Dibuje un cuadrado alrededor de la oreja.*

Draw an oval around the foot.   *Dibuje un óvalo alrededor del pie.*

Draw a rectangle around the nose.   *Dibuje un rectángulo alrededor de la nariz.*

Draw a star on the stomach.   *Dibuje una estrella sobre el estómago.*

Draw a circle around the hand.   *Dibuje un círculo alrededor de la mano.*

Draw a square around the eye.   *Dibuje un cuadrado alrededor del ojo.*

Draw a rectangle around the arm.   *Dibuje un rectángulo alrededor del brazo.*

DOT-TO-DOT

ditto

Teacher passes out dot-to-dot body part.
Children discover which part it is.

HOW MANY   *¿Cuántos/cuántas?*

This is an add-on chant to the tune of "Old McDonald."

How many heads do you have?	*¿Cuántas cabezas tiene usted.*
I have _____one_____ .	*Yo tengo uno.*
How many hands do you have?	*¿Cuántas manos tiene usted?*
I have _____two_____ .	*Yo tengo dos.*
Hands two,	*Manos dos,*
Head one,	*Cabeza una,*
How many mouths do you have?	*¿Cuántas bocas tiene usted?*
I have _____one_____ .	*Yo tengo uno.*
Hands two,	*Manos dos,*
Head one,	*Cabeza una,*
Mouth one, etc.	*Boca una, etc.*

WHAT'S MISSING   *¿Qué le falta?*

Teacher draws three faces on board.
One face is missing an eye.
One face is missing the nose.
One face is missing the mouth.
At each picture the teacher asks: "What's missing?"

Children now draw four faces.	*Dibujen cuatro caras.*
The face is missing the nose.	*Le falta la nariz.*
The face is missing two eyes.	*Le falta dos ojos.*
The face is missing the mouth.	*Le falta la boca.*
The face is missing one ear.	*Le falta una oreja.*

GO TOGETHER   *Va con*

Teacher demonstrates the concept of "go together."

The hand and the arm go together.	*La mano va con el brazo.*
The leg and the foot go together.	*La pierna va con el pie.*
The nose and the face go together.	*La nariz va con la cara.*
The hair and the head go together.	*El pelo va con la cabeza.*
The fingers and the hands go together.	*Los dedos van con las manos.*
The teeth and the mouth go together.	*Los dientes van con la boca.*
Teacher asks: "What goes with the hand?	*¿Qué va con la mano?*
Child responds: "The arm."	*El brazo.*

HANDS

Open them, close them.	Ábranlas, ciérrenlas.
Open them, close them.	Ábranlas, ciérrenlas.
Open them, close them.	Ábranlas, ciérrenlas.
And put them in your lap.	Y pónganlas aquí.

MR. SNOWMAN   Señor Nieve

multicolored construction paper
precut white circles of two sizes, 2″ and 3″ in diameter
toothpicks
glue
Avery dots — blue, red, pink, orange
crayons

Teacher dictates:

Here is Mr. Snowman	Aquí está el Señor Nieve.
He has a head.	Él tiene una cabeza.
(Paste on smaller white circle.)	
He has blue eyes.	Él tiene ojos azules.
(Everyone takes two blue dots and applies them.)	
He has a red nose because it is very cold.	Él tiene una nariz roja porque hace mucho frío.
(Apply one red dot.)	
He has two ears. His ears are pink because it is very cold.	Él tiene dos orejas. Las orejas son rosadas porque hace mucho frío.
(Apply two pink dots.)	
Mr. Snowman has a big stomach.	Él Señor Nieve tiene un estómago grande.
(Paste on larger white circle and apply one orange dot for belly button.)	
Mr. Snowman wears a hat.	Él Señor Nieve lleva un sombrero.
(Draw on a hat.)	
Finish by drawing a smile on Mr. Snowman's face.	Tiene una sonrisa.
He has a new friend. Another Mr. Snowman.	Tiene un nuevo amigo. Otro Señor Nieve.
He is happy.	Él está contento.

RHYME

Put, put, put	Pon, pon, pon
the little finger in the belly button.	el dedito en el botón.

WIGGLE YOUR FINGERS

Wiggle your fingers,	Muevan los dedos,
Wiggle your toes,	Muevan los pies,
Wiggle your shoulders,	Muevan los hombros,
Wiggle your nose.	Muevan la nariz.

Now all the wiggles have gone from me,	Ya se fué la mueva de mí,
And I will be still — as still as can be.	Estoy quieto — así, así.

CATALONIAN NURSERY RHYME

I have o-o-o
a little ant in my belly o-o-o
that is tickling me o-o-o

and won't let me sleep.

Tengo o-o-o
una hormiguita en la barriga o -o -o
que me está haciendo
cosquillitas o-o-o
y no me deja dormir.

CLOTHESPINS

appliance box
clothespins
scissors

Make large cardboard man with arms outstretched.
Cut holes for eyes, nose, mouth, ears, knees, legs, arms, and feet.
Have child clip two clothespins in holes for eyes while saying:

"I have two eyes."　　　　　　　　　*—Tengo dos ojos.—*

Continue with other body parts.

WATCH WHAT I DO

Teacher models.
Children follow suit.

I see with my eyes.
I kiss with my lips.
I draw with my hands.
I walk with my legs.
I count with my fingers.

Yo veo con los ojos.
Yo beso con los labios.
Yo dibujo con las manos.
Yo camino con las piernas.
Yo cuento con los dedos.

I think with my head.
I listen with my ears.
I dance with my feet.
I smell with my nose.
I eat with my mouth.

Yo pienso con la cabeza.
Yo escucho con las orejas.
Yo bailo con los pies.
Yo huelo con la nariz.
Yo como con la boca.

Continue:
Teacher commands a child:
Eat with your mouth.
Listen with your ears.

Coma con la boca.
Escuche con las orejas.

Teacher adds variety:
Walk with your hands.
Draw with your nose.

Camine con las manos.
Dibuje con la nariz.

Continue:
Teacher commands child:
Eat with your mouth.
Teacher asks class:
What does he do with his mouth?
Teacher responds:
He eats with his mouth.

Coma con la boca.

¿Qué hace con la boca?

Come con la boca.

ONE, TWO OR MORE?

Teacher gives key word: ears

Teacher says:

Do you have one, two or more?
  Children respond:

I have **two** ears.

Teacher says and models verb:
to listen with.

Sample:

I have 2 (eyes) to see with.
I have 2 (legs) to walk with.
I have 1 (mouth) to eat with.
I have 1 (nose) to smell with.
I have 2 (arms) to hug with.
I have 2 (hands) to draw with.
I have 1 (head) to think with.
I have 10 (fingers) to count with.
I have many (teeth) to eat with.

¿Uno, dos a más?

orejas

¿Tiene uno, dos o más?

Tengo dos orejas.

para escuchar.

Tengo 2 (ojos) para ver.
Tengo 2 (piernas) para caminar.
Tengo 1 (boca) para comer.
Tengo 1 (nariz) para holer.
Tengo 2 (brazos) para abrazar.
Tengo 2 (manos) para dibujar.
Tengo 1 (cabeza) para pensar.
Tengo 10 (dedos) para contar.
Tengo muchos (dientes) para comer.

I CAN

Teacher models.
Children imitate.

I can look with my eyes.
I look, I look, I look.

I can touch with my fingers.
I touch, I touch, I touch.

I can jump with my legs.
I jump, I jump, I jump.

I can listen with my ears.
I listen, I listen, I listen.

I can taste with my mouth.
I taste, I taste, I taste.

I can smell with my nose.
I smell, I smell, I smell.

Yo puedo mirar con los ojos.
Miro, miro, miro.

Yo puedo tocar con los dedos.
Toco, toco, toco.

Yo puedo saltar con las piernas.
Salto, salto, salto.

Yo puedo escuchar con las orejas.
Escucho, escucho, escucho.

Yo puedo probar con la boca.
Pruebo, pruebo, pruebo.

Yo puedo holer con la nariz.
Huelo, huelo, huelo.

DIRECTIONS

Hands up,
Hands down.
Hands out,
Hands in.
Hands to the right,
Hands to the left.
Show me your hands.

Substitute:

tongue
glass

Manos arriba,
Manos abajo.
Manos afuera,
Manos adentro.
Manos a la derecha,
Manos a la izquierda.
Enséñeme las manos.

la lengua
el vaso

DON ELEFANTE

Choose stuffed animal.
Name him.
Use stuffed animal to illustrate:

kiss, hug, smile, cry   *besar, abrazar, sonreir, llorar*

Model kiss and hug.
Draw a smile on face with finger.
Rub eyes and sniffle for crying.

Teacher directs child:
Kiss Don Elefante.   *Bese Don Elefante.*
Hug Don Elefante.   *Abrace Don Elefante.*
Don Elefante smiles.   *Sonría Don Elefante.*
(Child draws smile.)
Don Elefante cries.   *Llore Don Elefante.*
(Child rubs his eyes.)

Continue:
Kiss Don Elefante with your lips.
Hug Don Elefante with your hands and arms.
Don Elefante smiles with his mouth.
(Child draws smile and points to own mouth.)
Don Elefante cries with his eyes.

Continue:
What do you use to kiss?   *¿Qué se usa para besar?*
What do you use to hug?   *¿Qué se usa para abrazar?*
What do you use to smile?   *¿Qué se usa para sonreir?*
What do you use to cry?   *¿Qué se usa para llorar?*

RIGHT OR LEFT?

white tag board cut into 8-1/2" x 11" size, two for each child
crayons

right hand   *la mano derecha*
right foot   *el pie derecho*
left hand   *la mano izquierda*
left foot   *el pie izquierdo*

Children trace hands and feet onto cards and color them for learning left and
    right.
Teacher says the following:
John, pass the right foot to Mary.   *Juan, pase el pie derecho a María.*
Mary, pass the left hand to Theresa.   *María, pase la mano izquierda a*
                                            Teresa.
Theresa, pass the left foot to Martin.   *Teresa, pase el pie izquierdo a*
                                            Martín.

Teacher continues until all children have passed something.
Then teacher asks, "Who has a right foot?" or "Who has a left hand?" until all the
    cards have been collected.

TWISTER

1 white shower curtain
8 permanent magic markers

White circle would be outlined in black.
Purple and pink will need to be colored on.
Draw circles 7" in diameter.
Space them evenly on curtain.

Variation:

1 white tablecloth
fabric crayons

Teacher calls children individually.

Place your right foot on green and your left hand on yellow.	Ponga el pie derecho sobre el verde y la mano izquierda sobre el amarillo.
Place both feet on red and your right hand on purple.	Ponga los dos pies sobre el rojo y la mano derecha sobre el violeta.
Place your left hand on blue and your left foot on grey.	Ponga la mano izquierda sobre el azul y el pie izquierdo sobre el gris.
Place both hands on brown and your right foot on white.	Ponga las dos manos sobre el pardo y el pie derecho sobre el blanco.
Place your right hand on pink and your right foot on pink.	Ponga la mano derecha sobre el rosado y el pie derecho sobre el rosado.
Place your left foot on black and your right hand on black.	Ponga el pie izquierdo sobre el negro y la mano derecha sobre el negro.

SONG

(Hokey Pokey)

Jenni Kotarski
E. Kentwood High School, MI

Put your right hand in	Pongan la mano derecha adentro
Put your right hand out	Pongan la mano derecha afuera
Put your right hand in	Pongan la mano derecha adentro
and shake it all about	Y muévansela
Do the hokey pokey and	Hagan el hokey pokey y
turn your self around	Den la vuelta así
That's what it's all about.	Bailen el hokey pokey.

Children stand in a circle.

On the line — **Do the hokey pokey and turn yourself around** the children raise and lower arms as they are turning.

On the line — **That's what it's all about** everyone claps and turns as they sing this line.

After all body parts have been mentioned, the song ends like this:

Do the hokey pokey **(raise and lower arms)**	Hagan el hokey pokey
the hokey pokey	el hokey pokey
That's what it's all about. **(clap and turn)**	Bailen el hokey pokey.

ACTIONS

Review the Total Physical Response Method outlined in Chapter II.

COLOR

Children color pictures from coloring books depicting different actions.

IDENTIFY

Children identify action flashcards.

PANTOMIME

Child pantomimes action. Class identifies action.

ROLE REVERSAL

Child is teacher and commands another child to perform an action.

PICK A CARD

Child picks one card from action cards held by teacher.
Child performs action on card.
Class identifies action.

BALL GAME

Teacher models the following action.
Child is chosen to perform action.
Sample: Roll the ball to Ana.

Throw the ball	Tire la pelota
Roll	Ruede
Bounce	Rebote
Pass	Pase

SITUATIONS

plastic glass, tray

Practical life experiences are fun.
Model each situation.
Call two children at a time to do situation.

Excuse me   *Perdóneme*
(Two children bump into each other.)

Glad to know you.   *Mucho gusto.*
(Two children shake hands.)

Careful   *¡Cuidado!*
(One child covers head as if something is falling. The other child says: Careful!)

Oops!   *¡Epa!*
(One child is waiter and accidentally spills milk on child being served.)

LISTEN AND PERFORM

Teacher models actions.
Children imitate.

Stand up.	*Levántense.*
Sit down.	*Siéntense.*
Stand up.	*Levántense.*
Walk.	*Caminen.*
Stop.	*Párense.*
Walk.	*Caminen.*
Stop.	*Párense.*
Turn around.	*Den la vuelta.*
Stop.	*Párense.*
Jump.	*Salten.*
Stop.	*Párense.*
Turn around and jump.	*Den la vuelta y salten.*
Stop.	*Párense.*
Jump and walk.	*Salten y caminen.*
Stop.	*Párense.*
Walk.	*Caminen.*
Stop.	*Párense.*
Sit down.	*Siéntense.*

CIRCLE FUN

Each child in group must do and say a different action.

I jump.	Yo salto.
I walk.	Yo camino.
I run.	Yo corro.
I sit down.	Me siento.
I stand up.	Me levanto.

RED LIGHT, GREEN LIGHT

The teacher is at the head of the class.
(This activity may be child directed later.)
The class forms a line facing the teacher at the opposite end of the classroom.
The teacher turns her back to the children.
The teacher then calls out a command in Spanish and says "Green light" or
　　—¡Adelante!—
Children perform the particular action while trying to tag the teacher out.
Suddenly, the teacher says "Red light" or —¡Párense!— and turns around quickly
　　to spot anyone still moving.
If the teacher catches someone the child is out of the game.
The game continues until someone tags the teacher.

Action words:

Dance	*Bailen*
Walk	*Caminen*
Skip	*Brinquen*
Twirl	*Den la vuelta*

56

RED ROVER

The class is divided into two teams.
The first person on one team chooses one person from the other team to come
  over.
This child comes over while performing an action commanded from the opposing
  team.
For example, —¡María, María, baila!—
Mary then dances all the way over to the other team.
If the child does not know what to do, he sits down and the team receives a
  penalty point.
The winning team has the least amount of penalty points.

DUCK, DUCK, GOOSE   Pato, Pato, Ganso

Children are seated in a circle.
Teacher proceeds to tap each head until she says —Ganso.—
The child whose head she has just tapped —Ganso— rises and performs an action
  which the teacher commands.
The action is done all the way around the outside of the circle.
The teacher resumes tapping heads.

CAT AND MOUSE   El Gato y el Ratón

This game reinforces the open/close concept.
Two children are chosen.
One child is the cat.
The other child is the mouse.
The class forms a circle and holds hands.
The mouse is outside the circle.
The cat is opposite the mouse on the other side of the circle.
Both children run around the circle once until they pass their starting place.
The object of the game is for the mouse not to be caught by the cat.
The mouse may go through the inside of the circle or run around the outside of
  the circle always keeping away from the cat.
As the mouse tries to get in the children throw their hands up and chant:
  —¡Abra la puerta!— or "Open the door!"
As the cat approaches the children throw their hands down and chant:
  —¡Cierre la puerta!— or "Close the door!"

*This activity is recommended for the playground.

SIMON SAYS

Chant:

Simon says do this,	Simón dice salten,
do this,	salten,
do this,	salten,
Just like me.	Salten como yo.

Substitute:

Touch	Toquen
Walk	Caminen
Run	Corren

BENDING MAN

I'm a bending,
    bending,
    bending man.
	Estoy doblando,
	    doblando,
	    doblando mucho.

I begin to get tired, I begin to get tired.	*Empiezo a cansar,* *Empiezo a cansar.*

But all I can do is
    bend,
    bend,
    bend.
	Pero todo lo que hago es
	    doblar,
	    doblar,
	    doblar.

I'm a bending,
    bending,
    bending man.
	Estoy doblando,
	    doblando,
	    doblando mucho.

Substitute:
point, jump, running in place.

ONE, TWO THREE

One, Two Three	*Uno, dos, tres*
We all clap at once.	*Aplaudamos a la vez.*
Four, Five, Six	*Cuatro, cinco, seis*
Kick.	*Echen a puntapíes.*
Seven, Eight, Nine	*Siete, ocho, nueve*
Nobody move.	*Nadie se mueve.*
And Ten	*Y diez*
We all jump at once.	*Saltamos a la vez.*

TWO BY TWO

Choose two children.
They perform action while remainder of group claps and sings.
On the last line the whole group performs the action.

Mary and Tom are
    jumping on the floor,
    jumping on the floor,
    jumping on the floor,
Mary and Tom are
    jumping on the floor,
and all the others want to jump.
	María y Tomás están
	    saltando en el piso,
	    saltando en el piso,
	    saltando en el piso,
	María y Tomás están
	    saltando en el piso,
	y todos los demás quieren saltar.

Substitute:
Other actions.

QUERY

Teacher commands: Mary, dance. Teacher asks class: What does Mary do? Class responds: Mary dances.	 *Baile María.* *¿Qué hace María?* *María baila.*

58

EXERCISE

Chant and perform

The little children march,	Los niñitos marchan,
march,	marchan,
march,	marchan,
in Spanish class.	en la clase de español.

Substitute:

listen	escuchan
speak	hablan
look	miran
sing	cantan
dance	bailan

FREEZING ACTIVITY

Play some lively music and command children to: walk, jump, march in Spanish. Children freeze when music stops until it starts again.

MOVEMENT

Clap your hands and stop your motion.	Aplauden, aplauden y párense.
Turn around and stop your motion.	Den la vuelta y párense.
Touch your knees and stop your motion.	Toquen las rodillas y párense.
Stomp your feet and stop your motion.	Muevan los pies y párense.
Everybody run, run, run around the mountain.	Todos corren, corren, corren alrededor de la montaña.
Everybody run, run, run around the mountain.	Todos corren, corren, corren alrededor de la montaña.
Everybody stop.	Todos párense.

SONG

Teacher chooses child volunteer.
Teacher gives key phrase.
Child performs while other children imitate and sing along.

Verse:

Frank plays the guitar.	Paco toca la guitarra.
Frank plays the guitar.	Paco toca la guitarra.
Oh, Frank you play so well.	Oh, Paco tocas tan bueno.
Frank plays the guitar.	Paco toca la guitarra.

PACO TOCA LA GUITARRA

Pa - co to - ca la gui - tar - ra

Pa - co to - ca la gui - tar - ra

Oh Pa - co to - cas tan buen - o

Pa - co to - ca la gui - tar - ra

Key phrases:

Frank plays the guitar.
Suzanne dances the zamba.
Matthew drives the car.
Connie walks slowly.
Bob marches around.

Paco toca la guitarra.
Susana baila la zamba.
Mateo maneja el coche.
Constancia camina despacio.
Roberto marcha alrededor.

DIRECTIONS

APPLIANCES BOXES

appliance boxes
grocery boxes

Teacher models three directions at a time.
Child performs.

Go inside the box.	*Vaya dentro de la caja.*
Go outside of the box.	*Vaya fuera de la caja.*
Walk through the box. Like this.	*Camine por la caja. Asi.*
Raise the box.	*Levante la caja.*
Put the box above your head.	*Ponga la caja arriba de la cabeza.*
Lower the box.	*Baje la caja.*
Put the box under your nose.	*Ponga la caja debajo de la nariz.*
Run around the box.	*Corra alrededor de la caja.*
Jump over the box.	*Salte sobre la caja.*

STACKING CUPS

Available from Discovery Toys.

Teacher models what color cup is above or below another.

CLINKING WINE GLASSES

Teacher models:
up, down, out, in
using the wine glasses.

arriba, abajo, afuera, adentro

AEROBICS

Teacher is aerobics instructor.

Jump, jump, jump.	*Salten, salten, salten.*
Turn around, turn around.	*Den la vuelta, den la vuelta.*
Kick, kick, kick.	*Echen a puntapíes, puntapíes, puntapíes.*
Run. (count to 15)	*Corren. (cuenten hasta quince)*
Walk. (count to 15)	*Caminen. (cuenten hasta quince)*
Stop. Breathe. (count to 15)	*Párense. Respiren. (cuenten hasta quince)*
Twirl your arms (15X)	*Giren los brazos. (quince veces)*
Cross over your toes (8X)	*Tóquense los pies en cruz.*
	en cruz.
	en cruz. (5X more)
Put your hands on your waist.	*Pónganse las manos en la cintura.*
Twist to the right. (3X)	*Tuerzan a la derecha. (tres veces)*
Twist to the left. (3X)	*Tuerzan a la izquierda. (tres veces)*
Twist forward. (3X)	*Tuerzan hacia adelante. (tres veces)*
Twist backwards. (3X)	*Tuerzan hacia atrás. (tres veces)*
Stop. Breathe. (count to 15)	*Párense. Respiren. (cuenten hasta quince)*
Sit down.	*Siéntense.*

61

ROAD MAP

masking tape
matchbox car

Make road map using masking tape on floor.

Child guides matchbox car through map as teacher directs him.
Good practice for:

forward,	adelante,
stop,	pare,
to the right/left,	a la derecha/izquierda,
around.	alrededor.

OBSTACLE COURSE

Teach concepts of walking forward, backward, to the right/left, around, etc.
  (Camine hacia adelante, atrás, etc.)
Blindfold a child.
Lead him through an obstacle course by using directions.

DRILL SARGEANT

Put the gun above,	Pongan la arma arriba,
below,	abajo,
out,	afuera,
in,	adentro,
to the side.	al lado.

JUMP

Salte:

over the chalk.	sobre la tiza.
to the side of the pencil.	al lado del lápiz.
on the paper.	en el papel.

CANDY

3 paper cups
1 candy

Child closes eyes.
Teacher places candy in or under a cup.
Child opens eyes and locates candy.
Teacher asks:

Is the candy in or out of the cup?	¿Está dentro o fuera de la taza?
Is the candy under or over the cup?	¿Está debajo de or arriba de la taza?

ANIMALS

animal crackers
coloring books with pictures of animals mounted on posterboard
Fisher Price farm and animals
Animal puzzles by Instructo
dimestore plastic animals
Montessori wooden continent map or paper replicas
animal stickers

The Farm	*La Finca*	**The Forest**	*El Bosque*
dog	*el perro*	rabbit	*el conejo*
cat	*el gato*	bird	*el pájaro*
cow	*la vaca*	squirrel	*la ardilla*
pig	*el cerdo*	snake	*la serpiente*
hen	*la gallina*	toad	*el sapo*
rooster	*el gallo*	deer	*el venado*
chicken	*el pollito*	owl	*el búho*
horse	*el caballo*		
duck	*el pato*	**Land and Sea**	*La Tierra y el Mar*
sheep	*la oveja*	fish	*el pez*
rat	*el ratón*	snail	*el caracol*
bull*	*el toro*	whale	*la ballena*
donkey*	*el burro*	seal	*la foca*
turkey	*el pavo*	turtle	*la tortuga*
goat	*el chivo*	dinosaur	*el dinosauro*

The Zoo	*El Zoológico*	**Continents**	*Los Continentes*
parrot*	*el loro*	Europe	*Europa*
gorilla	*el gorila*	Asia	*Asia*
tiger	*el tigre*	South America	*Súdamérica*
lion	*el león*	North America	*Norteamérica*
alligator*	*el caimán*	Antarctica	*Antártica*
elephant	*el elefante*	Australia	*Australia*
ostrich*	*el avestruz*	Africa	*África*
zebra	*la cebra*		

*Indicates animals which inhabit Spanish speaking countries.

		Insects	*Los Insectos*
hippopotamus	*el hipopótamo*	spider	*la araña*
giraffe	*la jirafa*	fly	*la mosca*
llama*	*la llama*	mosquito	*el mosquito*
monkey*	*el mono*	bee	*la abeja*
camel	*el camello*		
reindeer	*el reno*		
bear	*el oso*		
penguin*	*el pingüino*		
rhinoceros	*el rinocerante*		
leopard	*el leopardo*		

SONG

Old McDonald Had a Farm

Old McDonald had a farm
e-i-e-i-o
And on his farm he had a cow
e-i-e-i-o
With a moo, moo here
And a moo, moo there
Here a moo, there a moo
Everywhere a moo, moo
Old McDonald had a farm
e-i-e-i-o

El Granjero y La Granja

Un granjero tenía una granja
e-i-e-i-o
Y en su granja tenía una vaca
e-i-e-i-o
Por aquí un mu mu
Por allá un mu mu
Aquí un mu mu, Allá un mu mu
Por todas partes un mu mu
Un granjero tenía una granja
e-i-e-i-o

Substitutions:

un perro	*guau, guau*
un gato	*miau, miau*
un cerdo	*snorting*
una gallina	*clo, clo*
un gallo	*qui, qui, riqui*
un pollito	*pio, pio*
un caballo	*clip, clip*
un pato	*cuac, cuac*
una oveja	*maa, maa*
un ratón	*ii, ii*
un toro	*breathe through nose*
un pavo	*gaubel, gaubel*
un chivo	*nee, nee*

PERFORM

Jump like the kangaroo
  rabbit
  toad

Salte como el canguro
  el conejo
  el sapo

Bite like the alligator
(open and shut hands)
  mosquito
  bee
  shark
(thumb up, hand moving forward, open and close fingers)

Muerda como el caimán

  el mosquito
  la abeja
  el tiburón

Scratch like the monkey
  the lion

Rásquese como el mono
  el león

Walk like the penguin
  toad
  spider

Camine como el pingüino
  el pato
  la araña

Swim like the whale
(blow through mouth, spout water)
  fish
(open/close mouth)
  Tom

Nade como la ballena

  el pez

  Tomás

Sing like the parrot **(Polly want a cracker)** bird	Cante como el loro el pájaro
Eat like the squirrel **(raise hands to mouth, click teeth)** chicken **(head down, bobbing up and eating)**	Coma como la ardilla el pollo
Talk like the snake **(sssssssss)** dog sheep cow pig	Hable como la serpiente el perro la oveja la vaca el cerdo
Paint the zebra leopard tiger giraffe	Pinte la cebra (stripes) el leopardo (spots) el tigre (rayas) la jirafa (manchas)
Wash yourself like the cat **(lick paws)** elephant **(use arm as trunk and throw water on back)**	Lávese como el gato el elefante
Stand up like the dinosaur **(stand straight, move hand behind like tail)** bear **(walk with arms and legs outstretched)**	Levántese como el dinosauro el oso
Run like the horse **(use tongue to make clicking noise)** bull **(charge ahead with fingers for horns)**	Corra como el caballo el toro
Watch like the owl **(look from side to side and hoot)** deer **(look and put hands over head for antlers)** fly **(flap arms as wings and look ahead and behind)**	Mire como el búho el ciervo la mosca

DRAW

Draw an animal that is fast.	Dibuje un animal que es rápido.
Draw an animal that is slow.	Dibuje un animal que es despacio.
Draw an animal that is tall.	Dibuje un animal que es alto.
Draw an animal that is short.	Dibuje un animal que es bajo.
Draw an animal that is intelligent.	Dibuje un animal que es inteligente.
Draw an animal that is stupid.	Dibuje un animal que es estúpido.
Draw an animal that is big.	Dibuje un animal que es grande.
Draw an animal that is small.	Dibuje un animal que es pequeño.

DESCRIBE ME

animal pictures
descriptive words

tall/short	*alto/bajo*
big/little	*grande/pequeño*
strong/weak	*fuerte/débil*
fast/slow	*rápido/despacio*
young/old	*joven/viejo*
smart/stupid	*inteligente/estúpido*

Which is slower?   *¿Cuál es más despacio?*
  tiger or turtle
  lion or snail
  spider or mosquito

Which is smaller?   *¿Cuál es más pequeño?*
  elephant or mouse
  llama or bee
  horse or sheep

Which is not smart?   *¿Cuál no es inteligente?*
  pig or cat
  leopard or chicken

Which is younger?   *¿Cuál es más joven?*
  chicken or chick
  dog or puppy
  cat or kitten
  sheep or lamb

Which is shorter?   *¿Cuál es más bajo?*
  dinosaur or giraffe
  llama or bear

Which is weaker?   *¿Cuál es más débil?*
  lion or sheep
  alligator or fish
  whale or shark

Illustrate strong/weak by showing muscles.
Illustrate smart/stupid by imitating dog standing and begging.

ADD-ON

I am going to the zoo.	*Voy al zoológico.*
I see: (first child)	*Veo:*
the monkey.	*el mono.*
I see: (second chlid)	*Veo:*
the monkey and the lion.	*el mono y el león.*
I see: (third child)	*Veo:*
the monkey, the lion, and the tiger,	*el mono, el león, el tigre.*
etc.	

WATCH ME

Teacher models verbs:

to feed	*dar de comer a*
to look at	*mirar*
to love	*querer*
to play	*jugar*

I feed the animals	*Le doy de comer a los animales.*
I look at the animals.	*Miro los animales.*
I love the animals.	*Quiero a los animales.*
I play with the animals.	*Juego con los animales.*

Teacher commands:

Feed the bird.	*Déle de comer al pájaro.*
Look at the tiger.	*Mire el tigre.*
Love the dog.	*Quiera al perro.*
Play with the monkey.	*Juegue con el mono.*

Stuffed animals are good for this activity.

SONG

(Farmer In The Dell tune)

The tiger in the jungle	*El tigre en la selva*
The tiger in the jungle	*El tigre en la selva*
Look! Listen!	*¡Miren! ¡Escuchen!*
The tiger in the jungle	*El tigre en la selva*

Substitute:

lion
giraffe
monkey
elephant
snake

Variation:
Habitat vocabulary

bird/nest	*el pájaro/el nido*
whale/sea	*la ballena/el mar*
cow/country	*la vaca/el campo*
worm/ground	*el gusano/el suelo*
tiger/jungle	*el tigre/la selva*
camel/desert	*el camello/el desierto*

Teacher places pictures of animals and habitats on chalkboard.
Teacher points to each as children sing Farmer in the Dell song.

THE HOUSE

Teacher discusses the word "house" with the children.
House books are made.
The cover is a pre-cut simple shape of a house.
The contents are plain white pages.

Teacher says the following sentences.
Children draw accordingly.

Page 1:
The nest is a house for birds.

El nido es una casa para los pájaros.

Page 2:
The sea is a house for fish.

El mar es una casa para los peces.

Page 3:
The ground is a house for worms.

El suelo es una casa para los gusanos.

Page 4:
The zoo is a house for animals.

El zoológico es una casa para los animales.

Page 5:
The barn is a house for horses.

El granero es una casa para los caballos.

Page 6:
The cave is a house for bats.

La cueva es una casa para los murciélagos.

GUESS WHO

Have children draw imaginary animals.
Teacher then describes the animals.
Later, children describe their animals.

Sample:
It is small.

Es pequeño.

It likes worms.

Le gustan los gusanos.

It lives in a nest.

Vive en un nido.

It sings well.

Canta bien.

It is a bird.

Es un pájaro.

EYES

Teacher draws one pair of interesting eyes on a ditto.
She instructs children to draw an animal using the eyes.
Class compares animals while teacher asks: What animal is it?

WHAT IS IT?

animal pictures

Teacher asks children:
Is this animal a lion or a bear, etc.

¿Es este animal un león o un oso?

BODY PARTS

Teach animal body parts.

beak	el pico
leg	la pata
wing	la ala
trunk	la trompa
fur	la piel
tail	la cola

Teacher gives examples of animal body parts.

The dog has four legs.	El perro tiene cuatro patas.
The horse has a tail.	El caballo tiene una cola.
The chicken has a beak.	El pollo tiene un pico.
The elephant has a trunk.	El elefante tiene una trompa.
The bird has a wing.	El pájaro tiene una ala.

Teacher discusses the concept of "is like," using pictures of the following:	és como

The animal leg is like your leg.	La pata es como la pierna.
The wing is like an arm.	La ala es como el brazo.
The trunk is like a nose.	La trompa es como la nariz.
The beak is like a mouth.	El pico es como la boca.
The fur is like the hair.	La piel es como el pelo.

LIKES

animal pictures

Introduce the verb: to like	¿Le gusta?

Which do you like more, the lion or the bear?	¿Qué le gusta más, el león o el tigre?

    the spider or the bee?
    the cow or the pig?
    the shark or the whale?
    the bird or the squirrel?
    the alligator or the gorilla?

MODELING CLAY

Use in small groups.
Give each child some clay.
Each child makes a different animal.

READ

Una Función de Títeres by Troll Associates
Un Dinosauro en Peligro
Federico el Sapo

CHARADES

One child volunteers to walk like and talk like a particular animal.
Class then guesses which animal it is.

SONG

(Farmer In The Dell tune)

The mother of the house	*La madre de la casa*
The mother of the house	*La madre de la casa*
Stand up right now	*Levántese ahora*
The mother of the house	*La madre de la casa*

Substitutions:

the father	*el padre*
the dog	*el perro*
the cat	*el gato*
the cheese	*el queso*
the family	*la familia*

Children are seated in a circle.

5 volunteers are needed to play each of the above parts.

When child's part is called he goes to the middle of the circle, claps with whole class and turns around.

On the last line, the remaining children tap the heads of those in the center of the circle as they are singing.

FINGERPLAY

Tomás Chavez

Eeency-Weency Spider	*La Arañita*
The eency-weency spider	*La arañita sube*
climbed up the water spout.	*alto, alto sí.*
Down came the rain and	*Llueve y lava*
washed the spider out.	*la arañita sí.*
Out came the sun and	*Sale el sol y*
dried up all the rain. And	*seca todo sí y*
the eency-weency spider	*la arañita sube*
went up the spout again.	*alto, alto sí.*

Actions:

1. Put fingertips together and bend them up and down as hands are raised slowly into the air.
2. Use fingers to indicate rain falling down.
3. Use "out" motion in sports.
4. Raise arms together above head to form sun.
5. Pretend to dry something.
6. Repeat actions of line 1 again.

HOT POTATO

Pictures of animals are placed in a paper lunch bag.

Bag is passed until teacher calls time out.

Child holding the bag identifies animal he has selected.

Variation:

Four plastic or puzzle animals are passed in a staggered fashion.

Teacher shakes tambourine.

When tambourine stops all children holding an animal need to identify it.

CHANT

Come to see my farm that is beau-ti-ful.	*Vengan a ver mi gran-ja que es her-mo-sa.*
Come to see my farm that is beau-ti-ful.	*Vengan a ver mi gran-ja que es her-mo-sa.*
And the duck does this quack, quack.	*Y el pato hace así cuac, cuac.*

Continue with farm animals and their sounds.

CUANDO LAS VACAS SE LEVANTAN

Cuan - do las va - cas se le - van - tan ya se di - cen Ho - la.

Cuan - do las va - cas se le - van - tan ya se di - cen Ho - la.

mu mu mu mu Esto es lo que di - cen.

mu mu mu mu Esto es lo que di - cen.

LOOK AND SEE

Teacher places 3-4 animals on floor.
Children close eyes.
Teacher takes one picture or animal away and mixes up remaining animals.
Children open eyes and decide what's missing. *¿Qué falta?*

BEAN BAG TOSS

1 bean bag
4 separate poster boards
1 board each for domestic or farm animals, land and sea animals, zoo or wild
  animals and animals in nature.
Pictures are glued to board in random fashion.

Child volunteers to toss bean bag.
He stands up, closes eyes and tosses the bag.
The child identifies the animal under the bean bag.

CONCENTRATION

7 animal pictures are placed face up on the floor while children have eyes closed.
7 continent cut-outs cover the animal pictures.
Children open eyes and identify continent and animal.

ALPHABET ANIMALS

Dígame un animal que empieza con . . .

Teacher asks children to give her the name of an animal that begins with the letter
"l" for example.

a — la abeja, la ardilla, el avestruz
b — la ballena, el burro, el búho
c — el cerdo, el caballo, el chivo, el caimán, la cebra, el camello, el conejo,
     el caracol
d — el dinosauro
e — el elefante
f — la foca
g — la gallina, el gallo, el gorila, el gato
h — el hipopótamo
j — la jirafa
k — el koala
l — el león, el loro
ll — la llama
m — el mono
o — la oveja, el oso
p — el pato, el pavo, el pingüino, el pájaro, el pez, el pollito
r — el ratón, el reno, el rinocerante
s — la serpiente, el sapo
t — el toro, el tigre, la tortuga
v — la vaca, el venado

ANIMALS AND CONTINENTS

construction paper cut-outs of continents
plastic animals or animal pictures

África — el león, el elefante, la jirafa, el hipopótamo, la cebra, el gorila
Antártica — el pingüino, la foca
Australia — el oso koala, el canguro
Súdamerica — el caimán, la llama, el avestruz
Norteamérica — el loro, la vaca, el burro, el reno
Europa — el toro, la oveja
Asia — el tigre, la serpiente, el mono, el camello

Sequence

This is the tiger.	Este es el tigre.
And here is the continent of Asia.	Y aquí está el continente de Asia.
The tiger lives in the continent of Asia.	El tigre vive en el continente de Asia.
Touch the tiger.	Toque el tigre.
Touch the continent of Asia.	Toque el continente de Asia.
Put the tiger in the continent of Asia.	Ponga el tigre en el continente de Asia.

BINGO

See LINGO under "Colors."
Make bingo boards having 8 animals on each.
Teacher calls out animal.
Child needs to make Spanish sound of animal before covering space.

TALL MOUSE, SHORT MOUSE
(feltboard story)

El Ratón Alto y El Ratón Bajo

one feltboard
felt characters (one tall mouse, one short mouse)
felt things (a bird, spider, flower, grass, house, roof, rectangle for the floor, a few
    raindrops, a puddle, window, and a rainbow)

Once upon a time there was a tall mouse and a short mouse.
The mice were good friends.
When they saw each other the tall mouse would say to the short mouse, "Hi."
And the short mouse would say to the tall mouse, "Hi."

Había una vez un ratón muy alto y un ratón muy bajo.
Los ratones eran buenos amigos.
Cuando se veían el ratón muy alto le decía al ratón muy bajo —Hola.—

Y el ratón muy bajo le decía al ratón muy alto —Hola.—

The two friends walked together often.
While they walked, the tall mouse would say to the birds, "Hello, birds."

A menudo los dos amigos caminaban juntos.
Mientras caminaban el ratón muy alto les decía a los pájaros,
—Hola, pájaros.—

And the short mouse would say to the spiders, "Hello, spiders."
When they passed through a garden the tall mouse would say to the flowers, "Hello, flowers."
And the short mouse would say to the grass, "Hello, grass."
When they passed by a house the tall mouse would say to the roof, "Hello, roof."
And the short mouse would say to the floor, "Hello, floor."

Y el ratón muy bajo les decía a las arañas, —Hola, arañas.—
Cuando pasaban por un jardín el ratón muy alto les decía a las flores,
—Hola, flores.—
Y el ratón muy bajo les decía a la hierba, —Hola, hierba.—
Cuando pasaban por una casa el ratón muy alto le decía al techo,
—Hola, techo.—
Y el ratón muy bajo le decía al suelo,
—Hola, suelo.—

One day there was a storm.
The tall mouse said to the raindrops, "Hello, raindrops."
And the short mouse said to the puddle, "Hello, puddle."
Then they ran inside to dry off.

Un día había una tormenta.
El ratón muy alto les dijo a las gotas de lluvia, —Hola, gotas de lluvia.—
Y el ratón muy bajo le dijo a la poza,
—Hola, poza.—
Entonces los ratones corrían adentro para secarse.

"Hello, roof," said the tall mouse.
"Hello, floor," said the short mouse.
Soon after, the storm stopped.
The two friends ran to the window.
"Hello, rainbow," they said together.

—Hola, techo,— dijo el ratón muy alto.
—Hola, suelo,— dijo el ratón muy bajo.
Poco después cesó la tormenta.
Los dos amigos corrían a la ventana.
—Hola arco iris,— dijeron juntos.

IMAGINARY ANIMALS

Gene Lynch
Vandenberg Middle School
Lompoc, CA

pictures of Noah and his ark
body parts
descriptive adjectives
colors
continents
foods

Teacher introduces imaginary ark animals.

Once upon a time there was a man.
His name was Noah.
Noah had a big boat.
It was called an ark.
Today we are going inside the ark.
We are going to see the animals.
(Children are ushered to first area of the ark.)

Oh, look at the first animal.
This animal is very large.
Look at its nose.
The nose is very long.
This animal is grey.
This animal is very large.
Its nose is long and it is grey.

Look at the toes of this animal.
The toes are very big.
This animal likes children.
It carries children on its back.
This animal has big toes and likes
children.

Now, here is the second animal
(Children are ushered to second area of the ark.)
Look at its stomach.
The stomach of this animal is white.
The other parts of this animal are black.

This animal is white and black.
Its stomach is white.
This animal lives in the continent of
Antarctica.
It likes the cold weather and it likes the
water.
This animal lives in Antarctica in the
cold where there is water.

Había una vez un hombre.
Se llamaba Noé.
Noé tenía un barco grande.
El barco se llamaba un arca.
Hoy vamos dentro del arca.
Vamos a ver los animales.

Ay, miren el primer animal.
Este animal es muy grande.
Miren la nariz.
La nariz es muy larga.
Este animal es de color gris.
Este animal es muy grande.
La nariz es muy larga y este animal
es gris.
Miren los dedos de este animal.
Los dedos son muy grandes.
Este animal le gustan los niños.
Lleva los niños en la espalda.
Este animal tiene dedos grandes y
también le gustan los niños.

Aquí está el segundo animal.

Miren el estómago.
El estómago de este animal es blanco.
Las otras partes de este animal son
negras.
Este animal es blanco y negro.
El estómago es blanco.
Este animal vive en el continente de
Antártica.
Le gusta el frío y le gusta también el
agua.
Este animal vive en Antártica en el frío
y donde hay agua.

74

FOOD

La Comida

Vegetables · **Las Verduras**
beans · *los frijoles*
carrots · *la zanahoria*
potato · *la patata*
tomato · *el tomate*
corn · *el maíz*
onion · *la cebolla*
peas · *los chícharos*
lettuce · *la lechuga*
french fries · *las papas fritas*

Fruit · **La Fruta**
apple · *la manzana*
banana · *la banana*
strawberry · *la fresa*
pear · *la pera*
orange · *la naranja*
grapes · *las uvas*
lemon · *el limón*
pineapple · *la piña*
melon · *el melocotón*
watermelon · *la sandía*
cherry · *la cereza*
peach · *el durazno*

Groceries · **Los Comestibles**
butter · *la mantequilla*
bread · *el pan*
salt · *la sal*
pepper · *la pimienta*
cheese · *el queso*
oil · *el aceite*
noodles · *los tallarines*
rice · *el arroz*
sandwich · *el sandwich*
mustard · *la mostaza*
mayonnaise · *la mayonesa*
catsup · *salsa de tomate*

Meat · **La Carne**
chicken · *el pollo*
beefsteak · *el biftec*
ham · *el jamón*
hamburger · *la hamburguesa*
hot dog · *el perro caliente*
turkey · *el pavo*
fish · *el pescado*
seafood dish · *la paella*

Beverages · **Las Bebidas**
7-up · *7-up*
Crush · *Crush*
Coca-Cola · *Coca-Cola*
wine · *el vino*
beer · *la cerveza*
milk · *la leche*
tea · *el té*
coffee · *el café*
water · *el agua*
lemonade · *la limonada*

Dessert · **El Postre**
custard · *el flan*
ice cream · *el helado*
pie · *el pastel*
cake · *la torta*
cookies · *las galletitas*

Meals · **Las Comidas**
breakfast · *el desayuno*
lunch · *el almuerzo*
dinner · *la cena*
tea time · *la merienda*

*See "Holidays/Culture for food recipes.

LINGO

This is a variation of "Bingo."
When a food item is called and the child has it on his card, he says in target language, "I like it," or "I don't like it."

79

HOT POTATO

Plastic foods are placed in a bag and passed until the teacher says Stop.
A food is then selected by the child holding the bag and identified.

DRAW

Have children draw their favorite foods.
Discuss what they have drawn.

comida favorita

READ

Conteno Juan by Troll Associates

LISTEN AND PERFORM

Peel the carrot	*Pele la zanahoria*
the potato	*la patata*
the onion	*la cebolla*
the banana	*la banana*
the orange	*la naranja*
Stir the beans	*Revuela los frijoles*
the soup	*la sopa*
the eggs	*la huevos*
the rice	*el arroz*
the noodles	*los tallarines*
Wash the strawberries	*Lave las fresas*
the grapes	*las uvas*
the cherries	*las cerezas*
Cut the cake	*Corte la torta*
the meat	*la carne*
the watermelon	*la sandía*
the cheese	*el queso*
the butter	*la mantequilla*
the sandwich	*el sandwich*
Squeeze the lemon	*Exprima el limón*
the orange	*la naranja*
Bite the apple	*Muerda la manzana*
the pear	*la pera*
the peach	*el durazno*
Pour the milk	*Eche la leche*
the water	*el agua*
the wine	*el vino*
the salt	*la sal*
the pepper	*la pimienta*
the oil	*el aceite*
Spread the butter	*Unte la mantequilla*
the mayonnaise	*la mayonesa*
the mustard	*la mostaza*
the catsup	*la salsa de tomate*

SONG

Pasa la banana

Pass the banana to the right	*Pasa la banana a la derecha*
to the right	*a la derecha*
to the right	*a la derecha*
Whoever has the banana	*Quien tiene la banana*
Sorry, sorry!	*¡Lo siento! ¡Lo siento!*
Now you eat the banana.	*Ya comes la banana.*

Substitute:

apple	to the left
orange	above
lemon	below
watermelon	
grapes	
strawberries	

PASA LA BANANA

Pa - sa la ba - na - na a la de re cha

a la de - re - cha a la de - re - cha

Qui - en ti - ene la ba - na - na ¡Lo si - en - to!

¡Lo si - en - to! Ya co - mes la ba - na - na.

WATERMELON

ditto of watermelon
real watermelon
pencils

Children eat a slice of watermelon.
They count the seeds in Spanish.   *las semillas*
They write the number of seeds on their paper.

Mi sandía tiene _____ semillas.

FRUIT   *La Fruta*

shower curtain
magic marker
fruit

Draw grid lines on curtain.
Have children bring in a piece of fruit.
Graph the following:

green fruit
yellow fruit
red fruit
purple fruit
orange fruit
pink fruit
long/short fruit   *largo/bajo*
big/small fruit   *grande/pequeño*
fruit with seeds   *con semillas*

Children can then cut and peel fruit for a salad.

BLINDFOLD   *Ojos vendados*

Teacher blindfolds child.
Teacher puts fruit in a bag.
Child touches the fruit and identifies it.

FOOD TASTING   *¡Pruebe la fruta!*

Children are seated in a circle.
One child is blindfolded.
Teacher selects a fruit for the child to taste and identify.

ADD ON

Teacher begins:
I go to the store   *Voy a la tienda*
I buy bread.   *Compro pan.*
Next:
I buy bread and milk.   *Compro pan y leche.*
Next:
I buy bread, milk, and ice icream. *Compro pan, leche y helado.*

THE SHARK
El Tiburón

Children are seated in a circle.
Each child holds a plastic food or food card.
Teacher leads the following movement:

Everyone pretends to get into a boat.
Everyone rows in cadence.
Teacher says: "Oh, my God, a shark!"
Teacher asks: "Who has a banana, etc. for the shark?"
Child having the food which the teacher has named, walks to a basket in the middle of the circle, which is the shark's mouth, and deposits the food.
When the shark has been fed the teacher says:
"Hurry, hurry," until all rowers have arrived at shore.
Everyone wipes their brow after being spared from the shark.

We're going to the ocean, we're going to the sea. **(Row in cadence)**	*Vamos al óceano, vamos al mar,*
We're going to the ocean, we're going to the sea.	*Vamos al óceano, vamos al mar,*
Oh, my God!	*¡Ay, Dios mio!*
A shark!	*¡Un tiburón!*
He is hungry.	*Tiene hambre.*
He needs food.	*Necesita comida.*
Who has a _____ ? **(food item)**	*¿Quién tiene una _____ ?*
Hurry! Hurry!	*¡Apúrense, Apúrense!*

FOOD BOOK

Teacher has five food categories on chalkboard, (meat, vegetables, fruit, dessert and drinks).
Children choose foods from each category and draw the food on the appropriate page in their books.
Books contain five pages.
Children may write: I like or *Me gusta* on each page.
Children discuss which foods they have drawn.

FRIO/CALIENTE

plastic foods

One child is selected to find a plastic food which is hidden in the room.
Child begins to walk towards something.
Class chants —*frío or caliente*— (hot or cold) as the child either approaches or moves away from hidden object.
Hot means child is getting closer to discovering food.
Cold means child is moving away from food.
When child discovers food he can then identify it and state its location depending on vocabulary acquired.

Children love this game.
Make sure search area is small enough to make a fast discovery.

MARKET

Teacher sets up market along chalkboard.
Each store is identified by a sign written on the board.
Foods pertaining to each store are underneath the sign on the ledge.
Teacher directs child to buy certain foods at each store.

Go to the bakery.	*Vaya a la panadería.*
Buy bread and cookies.	*Compre pan y galletitas.*
Go to the butcher's shop.	*Vaya a la carnicería.*
Buy turkey, chicken and steak.	*Compre pavo, pollo y biftec.*
Go to the grocery store.	*Vaya a la tienda.*
Buy beans and noodles.	*Compre frijoles y tallarines.*
Go to the fruit store.	*Vaya a la frutería.*
Buy apples, oranges and bananas.	*Compre manzanas, naranjas y bananas.*
Go to the vegetable store.	*Vaya a la verdulería.*
Buy carrots and corn.	*Compre zanahoria y maíz.*
Go to the ice cream store.	*Vaya a la heladería.*
Buy chocolate ice cream.	*Compre helado chocolate.*

HOUSE BOOK

See: The House under "Animals."

Teacher explains "house."
Children draw corresponding pictures on each page of their books and label
  stores.

1. The bakery is a house for bread.
2. The butcher's shop is a house for meat.
3. The grocery store is a house for groceries.
4. The fruit store is a house for fruit.
5. The vegetable store is a house for vegetables.
6. The ice cream store is a house for ice cream.

PANCHO CARRANCHO

Ramiro Garcia
Prospect High School
Saratoga, CA

Teacher hands a food card to each child.
She says:
Pancho Carrancho does not eat
bread.   *Pancho Carrancho no come pan.*
Teacher then points to a child.
Child must identify the food in his hand while continuing with the phrase:
Pancho Carrancho does not eat   *Pancho Carrancho no come pan pero*
bread, but he eats (bananas).   *come bananas.*
Teacher then points to another child to continue.

If a child misses a turn because he cannot identify his food card, then he receives a
  slip of paper.
At the end of the game all children with slips of paper must perform an action
  which the class commands.

MEAL

table setting
plastic or picture foods

Put the meat on the plate.	*Ponga la carne en el plato.*
Pour a little salt and pepper over the meat.	*Eche un poco de sal y pimienta sobre la carne.*
Take the knife.	*Tome el cuchillo.*
Cut the meat.	*Corte la carne.*
Put a potato near the meat.	*Ponga una patata al lado de la carne.*
Take the knife and the butter.	*Tome el cuchillo y la mantequilla.*
Spread the butter over the potato.	*Unte la mantequilla sobre la patata.*
Take the spoon.	*Tome la cuchara.*
Serve yourself some peas.	*Sírvase los chícharos.*
Put the peas to the right of the meat.	*Ponga los chícharos a la derecha de la carne.*
Take the glass.	*Tome el vaso.*
Pour a little wine in the glass.	*Eche un poco de vino en el vaso.*
Take the salad.	*Tome la ensalada.*
Pour a little oil over the salad.	*Eche un poco de aceite sobre la ensalada.*
Serve yourself some soup.	*Sírvase la sopa.*
Smell the soup.	*Huela la sopa.*
Take the spoon.	*Tome la cuchara.*
Taste the soup. Is it tasty?	*Prueba la sopa. ¿Es sabrosa?*
Take the fork.	*Tome el tenedor.*
Taste the salad.	*Prueba la ensalada.*
Take the fork and the knife.	*Tome el tenedor y el cuchillo.*
Taste the meat.	*Prueba la carne.*
Take the fork.	*Tome el tenedor.*
Taste the potato.	*Prueba la patata.*
Take the spoon.	*Tome la cuchara.*
Taste the peas.	*Prueba los chícharos.*
Take the knife.	*Tome el cuchillo.*
Serve yourself a piece of cake.	*Sírvase un pedazo de la torta.*
Take the cup.	*Tome la taza.*
Pour a little coffee in the cup.	*Eche un poco de café en la taza.*
Take the spoon.	*Tome la cuchara.*
Throw a little sugar in the coffee.	*Eche un poco de azúcar en el café.*
Take the milk.	*Tome la leche.*
Pour the milk in the coffee.	*Eche la leche en el café.*
Stir the coffee.	*Revuelva el café.*
Did you like your meal?	*¿Le gustó la comida?*

COMPARISONS

food flashcards of:
ice cream
milk
coca cola
orange juice
beer

soup
fried eggs
french fries
hamburger
toast
coffee

Teacher asks class:
Which is hot?
Which is cold?

¿Cuál está caliente?
¿Cuál está frio?

FLASHCARDS

Teacher shows a different food card to each child.
She asks:
Do you like watermelon?
Child responds:
Yes, I like it.
No, no I don't like it.

¿Le gusta la sandía?

Sí me gusta.
No, no me gusta.

A BALANCED MEAL

plastic food or pictures

table	*la mesa*
chair	*la silla*
napkin	*la servilleta*
glass	*el vaso*
cup	*la taza*
plate	*el plato*
spoon	*la cuchara*
fork	*el tenedor*
knife	*el cuchillo*

on top of	*encima de*
underneath	*debajo de*
inside of	*dentro de*

Teacher begins by directing child to set the table according to her directions.
Teacher then has specific plastic food items which are incorporated into the
  directions.
*Be sure the children know directions in their native language before proceeding in
  the target language.

Put the fried chicken on the plate.
Put the fork inside the glass.
Take the plate and put it on top of the glass.
Take the hamburger and put it underneath the glass.

Ponga el pollo frito encima del plato.
Ponga el tenedor dentro del vaso.
Tome el plato y póngalo encima del vaso.
Tome la hamburguesa y póngala debajo del vaso.

COURTESIES

fruit
cups
spoons
napkins

Teacher has fruit cups on tray.
She asks each child:
Would you like the fruit?   *¿Quiere la fruta?*
Child responds:
Yes/please or no/thank you   *Sí/por favor o No/no gracias.*
Teacher gives fruit cup to child:
What do you say?   *¿Qué me dice?*
Child responds:
Thank you.   *Gracias.*
Teacher says:
You're welcome.   *De nada.*

WHAT'S MY SIZE?

plastic food or pictures

Teacher queries children:
Which is bigger?   *¿Cuál es más grande?*
   the melon or the watermelon   *el melocotón o la sandía*
Which is smaller?   *¿Cuál es más pequeño?*
   the grapes or the peas   *las uvas or los chícharos*
Which is longer?   *¿Cuál es más largo?*
   the carrot or the banana   *la zanahoria o la banana*
Which is shorter?   *¿Cuál es más bajo?*
   the potato or the hot dog   *la patata o el perro caliente*
Which is taller?   *¿Cuál es más alto?*
   the pineapple or the pear   *la piña o la pera*

ANIMALS

animal and food pictures
chalkboard

Incorporate food into the teaching of animals.
Teacher displays corresponding food and animals on chalkboard ledge.
While pointing to each picture card, she says the following:

The cow eats grass.   **La vaca** come **la hierba.**
The whale eats fish.   **La ballena** come **los peces.**
The snake eats insects.   **La culebra** come **los insectos.**
The chicken eats corn.   **El pollo** come **el maíz.**
The tiger eats meat.   **El tigre** come **la carne.**
The bird eats the worm.   **El pájaro** come **el gusano.**
The duck eats bread.   **El pato** come **el pan.**
The elephant eats peanuts.   **El elefante** come **el maní.**
The money eats bananas.   **El mono** come **la banana.**
The rabbit eats carrots.   **El conejo** come **la zanahoria.**

THE TABLE

La Mesa

ditto with picnic table drawn on it
crayons

to one side	*al lado de*
on top of	*arriba de*
underneath	*debajo de*
around	*alrededor*

Directions:
Pick up the red crayon.
Draw a plate.
The plate is on the table.

Tome el creyón rojo.
Dibuje un plato.
El plato está en la mesa.

Pick up the blue crayon.
Draw a knife to the right of the plate.

Tome el creyón azul.
Dibuje un cuchillo a la derecha del plato.

The knife is on the table.

El cuchillo está en la mesa.

Pick up the yellow crayon.
Draw a spoon near the knife.
The spoon is on the table.

Tome el creyón amarillo.
Dibuje una cuchara al lado del cuchillo.
La cuchara está en la mesa.

Pick up the green crayon.
Draw a fork to the left of the plate.

Tome el creyón verde.
Dibuje un tenedor a la izquierda del plato.

The fork is on the table.

El tenedor está en la mesa.

Pick up the orange crayon.
Draw a glass above the knife.
The glass is on the table.

Tome el creyón anaranjado.
Dibuje un vaso arriba del cuchillo.
El vaso está en la mesa.

Pick up the white crayon.
Draw a napkin around the fork.

Tome el creyón blanco.
Dibuje una servilleta alrededor del tenedor.

The napkin is under the fork.
The napkin is on the table.

La servilleta está debajo del tenedor.
La servilleta está en la mesa.

Touch the plate.
Touch the fork.
Touch the napkin.
Touch the spoon.
Touch the knife.
Touch the glass.

Toque el plato.
Toque el tenedor.
Toque la servilleta.
Toque la cuchara.
Toque el cuchillo.
Toque el vaso.

Now we can eat.
The table is set.

Podemos comer ahora.
Está puesta la mesa.

RESTAURANT

Pass out menus.
Children select two things from each category.
They write their choices on a slip of paper.
Teacher collects papers.
The next day children see what they have ordered.

EL MENÚ

FRUTAS

Naranja $4.00
Banana 2.00
Piña-Sandía 3.00
Manzana 4.00

BEBIDAS

Café-Té 3.00
Leche 4.00
Cerveza 5.00
Vino 6.00
Limonada 4.00
Coca-Cola 5.00
Crush 5.00

ENSALADAS

Ensalada y tomates 8.00
Ensalada de Chef 10.00
(queso, jamón)
Ensalada de Frutas 10.00
(piña, plátanos, manzanas)

SOPAS

Gazpacho 8.00
Sopa de tomate 6.00
Sopa de arroz 6.00
Sopa de pollo 7.00
Sopa de carne y vegetales 8.00

CARNES

Pollo Frito $12.00
Arroz con Pollo 14.00
Pavo 10.00
Jamón 10.00
Biftec 16.00

VERDURAS

Zanahorias 4.00
Maíz 4.00
Chícharos 3.00

HAMBURGUESAS

Hamburguesa 'Grande' 10.00
(queso, tomate, lechuga)
Hamburguesa Ranchero 18.00
(queso, tomate,
 lechuga, huevo)

POSTRES

Torta 7.00
Pastel 8.00
(banana con crema, de manzana, de cereza)
Helado 4.00
(vainilla, chocolate, de fresas)
Queso con Fruta 6.00
Flan 4.00
Sopapilla 4.00

¡BUENOS DÍAS!

DESAYUNO CONTINENTAL
$23.00

Jugo de Naranja
Café
Té
Leche
Fruta

Tostada (mantequilla, jalea)
Buñuelos
Media Luna

DESAYUNO RANCHERO
$45.00

Jugo de (naranja, piña, tomate)
Fruta de la Estación
(fresa, sandía, melocotón, uvas, naranja, piña)

Huevos (dos) — fritos

Jamón o Carne (biftec)
Tostada
Papas Fritas

COLORS

construction paper
pencils

Make color books using each color page to illustrate appropriate foods.
For example:
On the red page draw an apple.   *En la página roja dibujen una manzana.*

red — apple, strawberry, cherry, tomato
yellow — banana, corn, lemon, pineapple, peach
green — pear, melon, peas
purple — grapes
brown — beans
white — potato, onion
pink — watermelon
orange — orange, carrot

FLAN

Make custard with the children.
Finish up with this chant:

I like milk.   *Me gusta la leche.*
I like bread.   *Me gusta el pan.*
But what I like most is custard!   *¡Pero lo que más me gusta es el flan!*

LECHE FLAN

Lita Bustillo
Howell, MI

1 large can evaporated milk
1 small can evaporated milk
8 egg yolks
1 cup sugar
1/2 cup caramel syrup
1 tsp. lemon rind or vanilla

Make caramel syrup by boiling 1 cup brown sugar and 1/2 cup water until carmelized. Pour into 1 quart mold.

Scald milk in double boiler 15 minutes.
Beat egg yolks. Add sugar, milk and flavoring. Pour into the mold.
Place the mold in a large pan filled with water. Bake at 350° for 1 hour or until the mixture becomes firm. Cool before removing from the mold.

SUN
El Sol

Attach center of sun to blackboard with the word "Food" or *comida* in capital letters.

Pass out sentences in Spanish written on yellow construction paper. *(rays of sun)*
Have children bring up appropriate ideas as you read them and attach sentences to board.
*Make sure the children can read sentences because they have heard the vocabulary often.

The food is hot.	*La comida está caliente.*
Food is tasty.	*La comida es sabrosa.*
My dad eats too much.	*Mi papá come demasiado.*
I like food.	*Me gusta comer.*
My mom is a good cook.	*Mi mamá es buena cocinera.*
I need food to live.	*Necesito la comida para vivir.*
Food has calories.	*La comida tiene calorías.*

STONE SOUP

pot, ladle, stone, water bottle, potato, carrot, onion, beans, salt and pepper

pour	*echar*
peel	*pelar*
cut	*cortar*
stir	*revolver*
taste	*probar*

Teacher assigns vegetables to children ahead of time.

Teacher: Once upon a time there was a man. The man was very hungry. So he said, I'm going to prepare a stone soup. Watch!
First, I need a pot (takes pot from knapsack).
Next, a stone (takes stone from knapsack).
Finally, a ladle (takes ladle from knapsack).

Teacher: Now I need a little water.
Child: I have the water.
Teacher: I pour a little water in the pot. — You pour a little water in the pot.
Child: (pours water)
Teacher: Good, I need a potato.
Child: I have the potato.
Teacher: Thank you. I peel the potato. — You peel the potato.
Child: (peels potato)
Teacher: I cut the potato. Like this. — You cut the potato.
Child: (cuts the potato)
Teacher: Now I stir the soup. — You stir the soup.
Child: (stirs soup)
Teacher: I need an onion.
Child: I have the onion.
Teacher: Thank you. I'm going to peel the onion. Like this. Continue peeling the onion.
Child: (peels onion)
Teacher: Good. Now stir the soup.
Child: (stirs soup)

LA ROPA

Clothing

hat	el sombrero
jacket	la chaqueta
overcoat	el abrigo
pants	los pantalones
shorts	los pantalones cortos
shirt	la camisa
blouse	la blusa
skirt	la falda
dress	el vestido
swimsuit	el traje de baño
sweater	el suéter
socks	los calcetines
shoes	los zapatos
boots	las botas
gloves	los guantes
mittens	los mitónes

Accessories

purse	la bolsa
watch	el reloj
earrings	los aretes
ring	el anillo
nylons	las medias
umbrella	el paraguas
handkerchief	el pañuelo
eyeglasses	las gafas
tie	la corbata
belt	el cinturón
scarf	la bufanda
necklace	el collar
bracelet	la pulsera

Verbs

Point	Apunte
Touch	Toque
Take	Tome
Fold	Doble

Put on	Póngase
Take off	Quítese
Tie/untie	Ate/desate
Button/unbutton	Abotone/desabotone

Tie:	the tie
	the handkerchief
	the shoes
	the nylons

Ate:	la corbata
	el pañuelo
	los zapatos
	las medias

Button:	the dress
	the blouse
	the shirt
	the sweater

Abotone:	el vestido
	la blusa
	la camisa
	el suéter

Fold:	the handkerchief
	the pants
	the scarf
	the socks

Doble:	el pañuelo
	los pantalones
	la bufanda
	los calcetines

SONG

(This Is The Way I Wash tune)

This is the way I wear the hat
the hat
the hat
This is the way I wear the hat
Here in the school.

Así llevo el sombrero
el sombrero
el sombrero
Así llevo el sombrero
Aquí en la escuela.

SONG

(The Bear Went Over The Mountain tune)

This is my blouse,
    my blouse,
    my blouse,
This is my blouse,
Tra-la-la-la-la-la

Esta es mi blusa,
    mi blusa,
    mi blusa,
Esta es mi blusa,
Tra -la -la -la -la -la

Continue:
my hat
my dress
my pants
my shirt
my socks

THE CLOTHES BAG

Place some unusual clothes in a large bag.
Direct a child to put on a piece
of clothing.   *Póngase la blusa.*
The child then says:
I'm wearing a blouse.   *Llevo la blusa.*

SONG

(This Is The Way I Wash tune)

Child is selected to perform.
He closes his eyes.
Teacher shows class an article of clothing.
Child opens eyes.
Song begins.

Mario gets up
    gets up
    gets up
Mario gets up
So early in the morning.

Mario se levanta
    se levanta
    se levanta
Mario se levanta
Por la mañana.

He puts on his shirt
    his shirt
    his shirt
He puts on his shirt
So early in the morning.

Se pone la camisa
    la camisa
    la camisa
Se pone la camisa
Por la mañana.

Continue:
  pants
  shoes
  socks

CHARADES

Children pretend putting on a piece of clothing.
Others guess which piece it is.

THE CLOWN

El Payaso

body parts
ditto of clown

1. Color the hair blonde.	*Pinten el pelo rubio.*
2. Draw 2 blue eyes.	*Dibujen dos ojos azules.*
3. Color the nose pink.	*Pinten la nariz rosada.*
4. Draw a big red mouth.	*Dibujen una boca que es grande y roja.*
5. Color the shirt orange.	*Pinten la camisa anaranjada.*
6. Draw a yellow tie.	*Dibujen una corbata amarilla.*
8. Draw red and white socks.	*Dibujen los calcetines rojos y blancos.*
9. Color the shoes purple.	*Pinten los zapatos violetos.*
10. Draw a green hat on the clown's head.	*Dibujen un sombrero verde en la cabeza del payaso.*
11. Color the hands white.	*Pinten las manos blancas.*
12. Draw a flower in one hand.	*Dibujen una flor en la mano.*

ONE OR TWO?

Name a piece of clothing: socks
Ask the child if you use one or two.
Child responds:

calcetines
¿Se usa uno o dos?
Se usa dos calcetines

one	two
hat	socks
jacket	shoes
pants	mittens
shirt	boots
dress	gloves

TRUE/FALSE

Dress a baby doll.
Teacher makes true/false statements about the clothing the baby doll is wearing.
If the statement is true the children say, *si.*
If the statement is false the children say, *¡Qué ridículo!*

CHANT

Ferndale Schools
Ferndale, Michigan

uno, dos . . . los zapatos
tres, cuatro . . . el vestido
cinco, seis . . . los calcetines
siete, ocho . . . el sombrero
nueve, diez . . . los guantes

Children are standing, imitating teacher.
Teacher begins by kicking one foot forward on *uno* and the other foot forward on *dos.*
On *los zapatos* the teacher bends down and taps the shoes.
Activity continues by kicking first one foot, then the other while chanting and pretending to put on the appropriate clothing.

GRAB BAG

Children are seated in a circle.

A bag of pictures is passed around and each child chooses one picture.

Teacher may need to review clothing with children first to see if they can identify the picture they are holding.

First child asks neighbor to the right if he is wearing the clothing that is in his hand, i.e.

Are you wearing a shirt?   *¿Llevas una camisa?*

WHO IS IT?

Teacher describes a child in the circle by first identifying whether the child is a boy or girl.

The teacher then says three things about what the child is wearing.

Child who guesses correctly has turn to say three things about a child in the circle.

CLOTHESLINE   *La Cuerda*

Hang clothes on line.

Ask following questions:

What comes before the pants?   *¿Qué viene antes de los pantalones?*
What comes after the blouse?   *¿Qué viene después de la blusa?*

SUITCASE   *La Maleta*

I take out   *saco*
I put in   *meto*

Who wants to take something out of the   *¿Quién quiere sacar algo de la*
suitcase?   *maleta?*

Child performs.
Childs say what he is doing.
I take out the . . .

VACATION

We're going on vacation to   *Vamos de vacaciones a la*
Florida/Alaska.   *Florida/Alaska.*

What do I need to bring?   *¿Qué necesito llevar?*
Child: I need . . .   *Necesito*

FASHION SHOW

I wear   *Llevo*

Three children at a time choose one item from the teacher's clothing collection.
They put it on and come out one by one and tell the class what they are wearing.

NOTE: Interesting clothing can be found at garage sales.
Be sure to use clothing that captures children's attention such as old hats with veils, rhinestones, etc.

BODY PARTS

What do you wear on your head?
Child: I wear a hat.

¿Qué lleva en la cabeza?
Llevo el sombrero.

Continue:

eyes	glasses
shoulders	sweater, overcoat, jacket
hands	gloves, mittens
arms	watch, purse, umbrella, bracelet
ears	earrings
legs	pants, nylons
body	dress
chest	shirt, blouse
fingers	ring
feet	socks, shoes
neck	scarf, tie, necklace
stomach	belt
chest	blouse, shirt

POLICEMAN, POLICEMAN

picture of policeman
clothing cards

Teacher passes out clothing cards to three children, i.e. brown pants, blue dress
and red hat.
Teacher chants the following:

Policeman, policeman
I lost my friend.
He is wearing . . .

Señor policía,
Perdí mi amigo
Lleva . . .

The object is to identify the child holding the appropriate clothing card.

Variation:
Chalkboard and colored chalk.
Teacher describes missing friend.
Child draws clothing on board using appropriate colored chalk.

Variation:
Mannikin
Child dresses mannikin and describes friend's clothing to class.

CHANT

Whoever is wearing a red dress,
    a red dress,
    a red dress,
Whoever is wearing a red dress,
Stand up right now.

Quien lleva un vestido rojo,
    vestido rojo,
    vestido rojo,
Quien lleva un vestido rojo,
Levántese ahora.

I SPY

Teacher displays clothing on floor.
Teacher then spies something beginning with the letter "p."
Children identify article of clothing.

I see, I see	*Veo, veo*
I see a little thing.	*Veo una cosita.*
The little things begins with "p."	*La cosita empieza con "p."*

SONG

(Farmer In The Dell tune)

body part vocabulary

The hands and the mittens,	*Las manos y los mitónes,*
The hands and the mittens,	*Las manos y los mitónes,*
Look, how swell!	*¡Miren que bien!*
The hands and the mittens.	*Las manos y los mitónes.*

Substitute:

the head and hat	*la cabeza/el sombrero*
the eyes and glasses	*los ojos/las gafas*
the shoulders and jacket	*los hombros/la chaqueta*
the arm and the watch	*el brazo/el reloj*
the ears and earrings	*las orejas/los aretes*
the legs and pants	*las piernas/los pantalones*
the body and dress	*el cuerpo/el vestido*
the finger and the ring	*el dedo/el anillo*
the nose and the handkerchief	*la nariz/el pañuelo*
the neck and the tie	*el cuello/la corbata*
the stomach and the belt	*el estómago/el cinturón*

WHERE DO YOU PUT

body parts

Teacher begins.
Children respond.

Where do you put gloves?	*¿Dónde se pone los guantes?*
You put them on the hands.	*Se pone en las manos.*

Continue:

Where do you put the hat?	on the head
the dress?	on the body
the boots?	on the feet
the pants?	on the legs
the belt?	on the stomach
the sweater?	on the shoulders

MAGAZINES

Have children cut out clothing from magazines.
Teacher shows two choices to a child and asks:

"Which do you like more?"	*—¿Qué te gusta más?—*
Child responds: I like _____ .	*Me gusta más _____ .*

DOLLS

body parts
clothes for dressing paper dolls, Barbie dolls or paper dolls.

Put on/take off	Póngase/quítese
Show me	Enséñeme

Put the pants in the baby's mouth.

Ponga los pantalones en la boca del bebé.

Take off the bathing suit from the baby's head.

Quíte el traje de baño de la cabeza del bebé.

Put the bathing suit on the baby's body.

Ponga el traje de baño sobre el cuerpo del bebé.

Show me two green socks.

Enséñeme dos calcetines verdes.

ADD-ON

I put on the sweater.	Me pongo el suéter.
I put on the sweater and the hat.	Me pongo el suéter y el sombrero.
I put on the sweater, hat and the coat.	Me pongo el suéter, el sombrero y el abrigo.

SHOPPING SPREE

numbers

I have $90.00	Tengo noventa dólares.
I buy . . .	Compro . . .

List clothing.

CLOTHES STORE

Teacher draws different clothing on chalkboard with price tags.
She asks how much each item costs.

How much does the blouse cost?

¿Cuánto cuesta la blusa?

Child responds:

The blouse costs _____ .

La blusa cuesta _____ .

Continue with other clothes.

SPENDING MONEY

Teacher displays clothing with price tags.
She pretends to buy and pay for the items.

I go to the store.	Voy a la tienda.
I buy a blouse.	Compro una blusa.
The blouse costs $12.00.	La blusa cuesta doce dólares.
I buy a skirt.	Compro una falda.
The skirt costs $15.00.	La falda cuesta quince dólares.
I buy shoes.	Compro los zapatos.
The shoes cost $20.00.	Los zapatos cuestan veinte dólares.
12 + 15 + 20 = 47.	Doce y quince y veinte son cuarenta y siete.
I pay $47.00	Pago cuarenta y siete dólares.

100

RED RIDING HOOD

Caperucita Roja

paper
crayons
Red Riding Hood picture
book

Teacher reads story pointing out key words.
Children draw 8 illustrated pictures and make a book.

Once upon a time there was a girl.	*Había una vez una muchacha.*
The girl had blonde hair.	*La muchacha tenía pelo rubio.*
The girl had blue eyes.	*La muchacha tenía ojos azules.*
And the girl wore a red cape.	*Y la muchacha llevaba una capa roja.*
Her name was Red Riding Hood.	*Se llamaba Caperucita Roja.*
*Draw Red Riding Hood.	***Dibujen Caperucita Roja.**

The girl wanted to visit her grandma.
The grandma had a house in the
woods.
*Draw the grandma in her house.

La muchacha quería visitar a su abuela.
La abuela tenía una casa en el
bosque.
*Dibujen la abuela en su casa.

So, the girl, who was Red Riding Hood,
walked through the woods.

Entonces, la muchacha, que se llamaba
Caperucita Roja, caminaba por
el bosque.

The girl carried some fruit for her
grandma.
The girl passed by a wolf in the woods.

La muchacha llevaba unas frutas para
su abuela.
La muchacha pasaba un lobo en
el bosque.

They said, "Good morning" to each
other.
*Draw Red Riding Hood and the wolf.

Se decían, —Buenos días.—

*Dibujen Capercucita Roja y el lobo.

The wolf was very hungry.
So he ran ahead to the grandma's
house.
He knocked on the door.
"Who is it?" said the grandma.
"It's me, Red Riding Hood," said the
wolf.
"Come in, my dear."
Then the wolf ate the grandma.
*Draw the wolf and grandma.

El lobo tenía mucha hambre.
Entonces corría a la casa de la
abuela.
Llamó a la puerta.
—¿Quién es?— dijo la abuela.
—Soy yo, Caperucita Roja,— dijo el
lobo.
—Pasa, mi hija.—
Entonces el lobo comió la abuela.
*Dibujen el lobo y la abuela.

The wolf put on the grandmother's
clothes.
He put on grandma's hat.
He put on grandma's dress.
He put on grandma's glasses.
And he sat in the bed.
*Draw the wolf in bed.

El lobo se ponía la ropa de la abuela.

Se ponía el sombrero de la abuela.
Se ponía el vestido de la abuela.
Se ponía las gafas de la abuela.
Y se sentaba en la cama.
*Dibujen el lobo en la cama.

Soon after, Red Riding Hood arrived at the grandmother's house.
Knock. Knock. Knock.
"Who is it?" said the wolf.
"It's me, Red Riding Hood."
"Come in, my dear."
*Draw Red Riding Hood knocking at the door.

Red Riding Hood looked at her grandmother.
She seemed a little different.
"Your ears are very big, grandma."

"The better to hear you with, my dear."
*Draw the wolf with big ears.

"Your eyes are also very big, grandma."
"The better to see you with, my dear."
*Draw the wolf with big eyes.

"But grandma, your arms are so long."
"The better to hug you with, my dear."

*Draw the wolf with long arms.

"Grandma, your teeth are very big."

"The better to eat you with, very quickly."
*Draw the wolf with big teeth.

Red Riding Hood began to scream.
"Help me. Help me."
At this moment a man was walking by the house.
He helped Red Riding Hood and killed the wolf with an axe.
Now everything is fine.
*Draw a man with an axe.

Poco después Caperucita Roja llegó a la casa de su abuela.
Tan. Tan. Tan.
—¿Quién es?— dijó el lobo.
—Soy yo, Caperucita Roja.—
—Pasa, mi hija.—
*Dibujen Caperucita Roja llamando a la puerta.

Caperucita Roja miró a su abuela.

La parecía un poco diferente hoy.
—Tus orejas son muy grandes, abuelita.—
—Para oirte bien, mi hija.—

*Dibujen el lobo con las orejas grandes.

—Tus ojos también son muy grandes.—
—Para verte mejor, mi hija.—

*Dibujen el lobo con los ojos grandes.

—Pero abuela tus brazos son tan largos.—
—Para abrazarte bien, mi hija.—

*Dibujen el lobo con los brazos largos.

—Abuela, tus dientes son muy grandes.—
—Para comerte más rápido.—

*Dibujen el lobo con los dientes grandes.

Caperucita Roja empezó a gritar.
—Ayúdeme. Ayúdeme.—
En estos momentos pasaba por la casa un hombre.
El hombre ayudaba a Caperucita Roja y mató el lobo con un hacha.
Ahora todo está bien.
*Dibujen un hombre con un hacha.

FAMILY

father	*el padre*
mother	*la madre*
sister	*la hermana*
brother	*el hermano*
grandpa	*el abuelo*
grandma	*la abuela*
aunt	*la tía*
uncle	*el tío*

appropriate pictures of family members from magazines
Barbie, Ken, Skipper dolls

FAMILY CIRCLE

magazines
scissors
glue
paper

Children cut and paste magazine people on paper.
An example might be: Jaclyn Smith.
Child then does show and tell for class.
This is my mamá, etc.

ADD-ON

to love	*querer*

I love my mother.	*Yo quiero a mi mamá.*
I love my mother and my father.	*Yo quiero a mi mamá y mi papá.*
I love my mother, father and brother, etc.	*Yo quiero a mi mamá, mi papá y mi hermano.*

WHERE IS THUMBKIN?

Fingerplay. See "Identity."
Teacher or child holds up family member card.

Where is father?	*¿Dónde está papá?*	(Holds up card)
Where is father?	*¿Dónde está papá?*	
Here he is.	*Aquí está papá.*	(Moves card forward)
Here he is.	*Aquí está papá.*	
Where is father?	*¿Dónde está papá?*	(Holds up card)
Where is father?	*¿Dónde está papá?*	
He is gone.	*Papá no está.*	(Hides card)
He is gone.	*Papá no está.*	

WELCOME   *Bienvenido*

A large posterboard house is made and placed on chalkboard.
Teacher welcomes each family member into the house.
Child walks up to the house with family member picture and enters through the door.

The mother on the bus
talks, talks, talks
talks, talks, talks
talks, talks, talks
The mother on the bus
talks, talks, talks
all day long.

The grandmother on the bus
screams "Oh, my God!"
    "Oh, my God!"
    "Oh, my God!"
The grandmother on the bus
screams "Oh, my God!"
all day long.

The grandfather on the bus
snores (snor-snor-snor)
snores, snores, snores
snores, snores, snores
The grandfather on the bus
snores (snor-snor-snor)
all day long.

The aunt on the bus
laughs, laughs, laughs
laughs, laughs, laughs
laughs, laughs, laughs
The aunt on the bus
laughs, laughs, laughs
all day long.

The uncle on the bus
drinks, glo, glo, glo
    glo, glo, glo
    glo, glo, glo
The uncle on the bus
drinks, glo, glo, glo
all day long.

La mamá en el bus
habla, habla, habla
habla, habla, habla
habla, habla, habla
La mamá en el bus
habla, habla, habla
Todo el día.

La abuela en el bus
grita —¡Ay, Dios mío!—
    —¡Ay, Dios mío!—
    —¡Ay, Dios mío!—
La abuela en el bus
grita —¡Ay, Dios mío!—
Todo el día.

El abuelo en el bus
ronca (snor ronca)
ronca, snor, ronca
ronca, snor, ronca
El abuelo en el bus
ronca (snor ronca)
Todo el día.

La tía en el bus
ríe, ríe, ríe
ríe, ríe, ríe
ríe, ríe, ríe
La tía en el bus
ríe, ríe, ríe
Todo el día.

El tío en el bus
toma glo, glo, glo
    glo, glo, glo
    glo, glo, glo
El tío en el bus
toma glo, glo, glo
Todo el día.

LA GENTE EN EL BUS

La gente en el bus va arriba y abajo
Arriba y abajo arriba y abajo la gente en el bus
va arriba y abajo to-do el día.

READ

Los Padres by Barron's Educational Series.
A delightful book about parents and their children.

BENDING MAN

See "Actions"

Substitute:

to kiss	*besar*
to hug	*abrazar*
to greet	*saludar*
to talk	*hablar*

Estoy besando,
besando
besando mucho.

Empiezo a cansar,
Empiezo a cansar,
Pero todo lo que hago es
besar,
besar,
besar.

Estoy besando,
besando
besando mucho.

SONG

I have a (dad) that loves me
that loves me, that loves me;
I have a (dad) that loves me
and his name is _____ .

Yo tengo un (papá) que me quiere,
que me quiere, que me quiere;
Yo tengo un (papá) que me quiere,
y su nombre es ___(Ricardo)___ .

Refrain:
(La Cucaracha tune)

that loves me, that loves me
that loves me with all his heart
that loves me, that loves me
that loves me with all his heart

que me quiere, que me quiere
que me quiere con todo corazón
que me quiere, que me quiere
que me quiere con todo corazón

Song can be repeated with "you have" or "we have."

Teacher gives key word which is a family member.
One child volunteers his dad's name.
Class substitutes name on line #4.

SONG

1st stanza: Mulberry Bush tune

We're going to a wedding
        a wedding
        a wedding
We're going to a wedding
And everyone is going to dance.

Vamos a una boda
        una boda
        una boda
Vamos a una boda
Y todos van a bailar.

2nd stanza: Mulberry Bush tune

Here comes the father
        the father
        the father
Here comes the father
To dance with the mother.

Ya viene el papá
        el papá
        el papá
Ya viene el papá
A bailar con la mamá.

3rd stanza: Farmer in the Dell tune

Mother and father
Mother and father
Look how they dance
Mother and father.

Mamá y papá
Mamá y papá
Miren como bailan
Mamá y papá.

4th stanza: Mulberry Bush tune

Here comes the brother
        the brother
        the brother
Here comes the brother
To dance with the sister.

Ya viene el hermano
        el hermano
        el hermano
Ya viene el hermano
A bailar con la hermana.

5th stanza: Farmer in the Dell tune

Brother and sister,
Brother and sister,
Look how they dance
Brother and sister.

Hermano y hermana,
Hermano y hermana,
Miren como bailan
Hermano y hermana.

Decide who will be each family member.
You will need a mother/father
        brother/sister
        grandma/grandpa
        aunt/uncle
        bride/groom (*novia, novio*)
All members form a receiving line at a wedding.
Call each member forward for the wedding dance.
Remaining children form a circle, clap and sing as wedding party is called to dance.

FEELINGS

I am happy.	*Estoy contento.*
I am sad.	*Estoy triste.*
I am angry.	*Estoy enojado.*
I am sick.	*Estoy enfermo.*
I am frightened.	*Tengo miedo.*
I am hungry.	*Tengo hambre.*
I am thirsty.	*Tengo sed.*
I am sleepy.	*Tengo sueño.*
I am hot.	*Tengo calor.*
I am cold.	*Tengo frío.*

HOW ARE YOU?

Teacher states feeling.
Children act out feeling.

Variation:
Child places face through posterboard with hole cut out in it.
Child expresses emotion.
Class identifies feeling.

HANDS

Teacher commands and models:

Draw a happy face on one hand.	*Dibujen una cara contenta en la mano.*
Draw a sad face on the other hand.	*Dibujen una cara triste en la otra mano.*

Teacher asks individual children, "Are you happy or sad?"
Child responds by showing the teacher one hand and stating his emotion for the
day.
Teacher may wish to tally the results on the chalkboard.

FEELINGS

Children color and identify feeling pictures from coloring books or dittos.

Children identify emotion flashcards.

TOUCH AND FEEL

fan	*el abanico*
pillow	*la almohada*
aspirin	*la aspirina*
mouth	*la boca*
handkerchief	*el pañuelo*
gloves	*los guantes*
eyes	*los ojos*
glass	*el vaso*
apple	*la manzana*
chair	*la silla*
coat	*el abrigo*
birthday cake	*la torta de cumpleaños*
teddy bear	*el osito*

Touch the apple. You are hungry.	*Toque la manzana. Tiene hambre.*
Touch the glass. You are thirsty.	*Toque el vaso. Tiene sed.*
Touch the pillow. You are sleepy.	*Toque la almohada. Tiene sueño.*
Touch the teddy bear. You are afraid.	*Toque el osito. Tiene miedo.*
Touch the coat. You are cold.	*Toque el abrigo. Tiene frío.*
Touch the fan. You are hot.	*Toque el abanico. Tiene calor.*

Touch the aspirin. You are sick.	*Toque la aspirina. Está enfermo.*
Touch the chair. You are tired.	*Toque la silla. Está cansado.*
Touch the gloves. You are angry.	*Toque los guantes. Está enojado.*
Touch the mouth. You are happy.	*Toque la boca. Está contento.*
Touch the handkerchief. You are sad.	*Toque el pañuelo. Está triste.*

WHY?   *¿Por qué?*

candles
book
water
food

Teacher models and commands children to do the following situations.
Teacher comments on each action.

Fight!	*¡Peleen!*
I am sad because I don't have a friend.	*Estoy triste porque no tengo un amigo.*
Blow out the candles.	*¡Soplen las velitas!*
I am happy because I am six years old.	*Estoy feliz porque tengo seis años.*
Grab your head!	*¡Agarren la cabeza!*
I am sick because I have a headache.	*Estoy enferma porque tengo dolor de cabeza.*
Drink the water!	*¡Tomen el agua!*
I am thirsty because I don't have water.	*Tengo sed porque no tengo agua.*
Eat the food!	*¡Coman la comida!*
I am hungry because I don't have food.	*Tengo hambre porque no tengo comida.*

PAPER WORK

directions:
up/down   *arriba/abajo*
right/left   *derecha/izquierda*

Teacher models and dictates:

Fold the paper into four parts.	*Doblen el papel en cuatro partes.*
The kitchen is in the lower right part. Here is the kitchen.	*La cocina está en la parte de abajo a la derecha. Aquí está la cocina.*
Draw a table, two chairs, a window with curtains, the refrigerator and a stove.	*Dibujen la mesa, dos sillas, una ventana con cortinas, la nevera y estufa.*
Above the kitchen is the bathroom. Here is the bathroom.	*Arriba de la cocina está el cuarto de baño. Aquí está el bano.*
Draw the bathrub, the sink, the shower and the toilet.	*Dibujen la bañera, el lavabo, la ducha y el baño.*
The living room is in the lower left part. Here is the living room.	*La sala está en la parte de abajo a la izquierda. Aquí está la sala.*
Draw a lamp, a couch, an armchair, and a television set.	*Dibujen una lámpara, el sofá, el sillón y la televisión.*
Above the living room is the bedroom. Here is the bedroom.	*Arriba de la sala está el dormitorio. Aquí está el dormitorio.*
Draw a bed with a pillow, a dresser, a mirror and the closet.	*Dibujen la cama con almohada, la cómoda, el espejo y el ropero.*

WHAT'S MISSING?   *¿Qué falta?*

Use plastic furniture or pictures.
Place three pieces of furniture in front of the children.
Review the furniture pieces.
Children close eyes.
Teacher takes away one, then two, then all three pieces, each time asking:
—*¿Qué falta?*—
Children respond.

FIND THE IMPOSTER   *¿Qué está mal?*

Teacher can dictate or show pictures.

Living room: couch, lamp, TV set, toilet paper
Kitchen: refrigerator, stove, table, couch
Bedroom: bed, pillow, closet, stove
Bathroom: shower, bathtub, toilet, bed

READ

Tell the story of The Three Bears in Spanish.
An easy reader is: **Los Tres Osos:** LTO Enterprises, Phoenix, AZ 85014.

Where's Spot? by Eric Hill, G.P. Putnam's Sons, New York.

CHANT

vocabulary

to eat	*comer*
to sleep	*dormir*
to speak	*hablar*
to wash up	*lavarse*

Teacher calls two children at a time to perform.
Class chants along.

Ed and Lucy want to eat in the kitchen,
    eat in the kitchen,
    eat in the kitchen,
Ed and Lucy want to eat in the kitchen,
But all the others don't want to eat.

Eduardo y Lucía quieren comer en la cocina,
    comer en la cocina,
    comer en la cocina,
Eduardo y Lúca quieren comer en la cocina,
Pero todos los demás no quieren comer.

Substitute:

Wash up in the bathroom.	*Lavarse en el baño.*
Sleep in the bedroom.	*Dormir en el dormitorio.*
Talk in the living room.	*Hablar en la sala.*

BENDING MAN

See "Actions."

I am sleeping
    sleeping
    sleeping now.
I begin to wake up,
I begin to wake up,
But all I do is
    sleep
    sleep
    sleep
I am sleeping
    sleeping
    sleeping now.

Estoy durmiendo
    durmiendo
    durmiendo ya.
Empiezo a despertar
Empiezo a despertar
Pero todo lo que hago es
    dormir
    dormir
    dormir
Estoy durmiendo
    durmiendo
    durmiendo ya.

Substitute:

to snore/wake up	*roncar*
to eat/get tired	*comer/empiezo a cansar*
to drink/get tired	*beber*
to wash up	*lavarse*
to speak	*hablar*

IDENTIFICATION

Discuss city, street and phone number.

to live	*vivir*
city	*la ciudad*
street	*la calle*
phone number	*número de teléfono*

I live in the city of Howell, on the street, Mercado.
My phone number is 548-3517.

Vivo en la ciudad de Howell, en la calle Mercado.
Mi número de teléfono es 548-3517.

IN OR OUT?

outside	*afuera*
inside	*adentro*

The flower is inside or outside?	*La flor está ¿afuera o adentro?*
The lamp is inside or outside?	*La lámpara está ¿afuera o adentro?*
The table is inside or outside?	*La mesa está ¿afuera o adentro?*
The tree is inside or outside?	*El árbol está ¿afuera o adentro?*
The grass is inside or outside?	*La hierba está ¿afuera o adentro?*
The bed is inside or outside?	*La cama está ¿afuera o adentro?*
The sidewalk is inside or outside?	*La acera está ¿afuera o adentro?*

inside of	*dentro de*
outside of	*fuera de*

Teacher draws a house, refrigerator and a toilet on the chalkboard.
Teacher directs child:

The toilet paper is in the refrigerator.	*El papel higiénico está dentro de la nevera.*
The newspaper is in the toilet.	*El periódico está dentro del baño.*
The bed is outside the house.	*La cama está fuera de la casa.*
The couch is outside the house.	*El sofá está fuera de la casa.*

Child walks up to board and places picture card accordingly.

FLASHCARDS

house furnishings

on top of/underneath	*encima de/debajo de*

Put the lamp on the couch.	*Ponga la lámpara encima del sofá.*
Put the newspaper under the table.	*Ponga el periódico debajo de la mesa.*
Put the chair on the stove.	*Ponga la silla encima de la estufa.*
Put the pillow under the bed.	*Ponga la almohada debajo de la cama.*

Incorporate other vocabulary, i.e.
Put the tiger on the chair.

Ponga el tigre en la silla.

HOUSE BOOK

See "Animals."

Children draw one idea per page.

The garage is a house for a car.	*El garaje es una casa para el coche.*
The refrigerator is a house for food.	*La nevera es una casa para la comida.*
The closet is a house for clothes.	*El ropero es una casa par la ropa.*
The garden is a house for flowers.	*El jardín es una casa para las flores.*

WHERE DOES ONE FIND . . .?   *¿Dónde se encuentra . . .?*

Teacher gives key word.
Children respond with appropriate room in the house.

clothes/bedroom	*la ropa/el dormitorio*
food/kitchen	*la comida/la cocina*
television/living room	*la televisión/la sala*
toilet paper/bathroom	*papel higiénico/el baño*

Teacher gives key sentence.
Children respond with appropriate room.

Where one washes his body/ bathroom	*donde se lava el cuerpo/el baño*
Where one eats food/kitchen	*donde se come la comida/la cocina*
Where one watches TV/living room	*donde mira la televisión/la sala*
Where one sleeps/bedroom	*donde se duerme en la cama/ el dormitorio*

Continue:

Teacher gives key sentence.
Teacher draws four objects on board; stove, closet, bed, sink
Children respond with appropriate object.

Where the food is prepared/stove	*donde se prepara la comida/la estufa*
Where the clothes are put/closet	*donde se pone la ropa/el ropero*
Where Tom sleeps/bed	*donde se duerme Tomás/la cama*
Where one washes his face/sink	*donde se lava la cara/el lavabo*

IS USED FOR

Teacher reviews "is used for" or —*se usa para.*—
Teacher attaches pictures to chalkboard.
Teacher begins sentence:

The lamp is used for reading. **(Children fill in missing object.)**	*Se usa (la lámpara) para leer.*

The armchair is used for sitting.	*Se usa (el sillón) para sentarse.*
The plate is used for eating.	*Se usa (el plato) para comer.*
The glass is used for drinking.	*Se usa (el vaso) para beber.*
The stove is used for preparing food.	*Se usa (la estufa) para preparar la comida.*
The shower is used for bathing.	*Se usa (la ducha) para lavarse.*
The bed is used for sleeping.	*Se usa (la cama) para dormir.*
The mirror is used for looking at.	*Se usa (el espejo) para mirar.*

CLASSROOM

La Clase

chalkboard	*la pizarra*	map	*el mapa*
chalk	*la tiza*	piano	*el piano*
pencil	*el lápiz*	clock	*el reloj*
crayons	*los creyones*	calendar	*el calendario*
scissors	*las tijeras*	book	*el libro*
eraser	*el borrador, la goma*	flashcards	*las tarjetas*
ruler	*la regla*	notebook	*el cuaderno*
paper	*el papel*	closet	*el ropero*
flag	*la bandera*	teacher	*el maestro/la maestra*
desk	*el escritorio*	student	*el alumno/la alumna*

VERBS

to open	*abrir*	to listen	*escuchar*
to close	*cerrar*	to watch	*mirar*
to point	*apuntar*	to repeat	*repetir*
to touch	*tocar*	to show	*enseñar*
to put in	*meter*	to tell	*decir*
to take out	*sacar*	to draw	*dibujar*
to take	*tomar*	to sing	*cantar*
to erase	*borrar*		
to glue	*pegar*		
to color	*colorar*		
to write	*escribir*		
to read	*leer*		
to cut	*cortar*		
to count	*contar*		

ACTIONS

Sit on the desk.	*Siéntese en el escritorio.*
Sit on the map.	*Siéntese en el mapa.*
Sit on the piano.	*Siéntese en el piano.*
Sit on the flag.	*Siéntese en la bandera.*
Run to the calendar.	*Corre al calendario.*
Touch the number 22.	*Toque el número veintídos.*
Jump to the flag.	*Salte a la bandera.*
Touch the blue part of the flag.	*Toque la parte azul de la bandera.*
Walk to the map.	*Camine al mapa.*
Show me Michigan.	*Enséñeme Michigan.*
Go to your desk.	*Vaya a su escritorio.*
Take out scissors, crayons and paper.	*Saque las tijeras, creyones y papel.*

WHAT'S MISSING

| Teacher: | I have the chalkboard. | *Tengo la pizarra.* |
| Child: | I'm missing the chalk. | *Me falta la tiza.* |

| Teacher: | I have the paper. | *Tengo el papel.* |
| Child: | I'm missing the pencil. | *Me falta el lápiz.* |

| Teacher: | I have the teacher. | *Tengo la maestra.* |
| Child: | I'm missing the student. | *Me falta el alumno.* |

| Teacher: | I have the scissors. | *Tengo las tijeras.* |
| Child: | I'm missing the paper. | *Me falta el papel.* |

| Teacher: | I have the clock. | *Tengo el reloj.* |
| Child: | I'm missing the hour. | *Me falta la hora.* |

Variation:

| Teacher: | I want to write. | *Quiero escribir.* |
| Child: | I'm missing the (pencil). | *Me falta el lápiz.* |

| Teacher: | I want to read. | *Quiero leer.* |
| Child: | I'm missing the (book). | *Me falta el libro.* |

| Teacher: | I want to sing. | *Quiero cantar.* |
| Child: | I'm missing the (music). | *Me falta la música.* |

| Teacher: | I want to paint. | *Quiero pintar.* |
| Child: | I'm missing the (paint). | *Me falta la pinta.* |

| Teacher: | I want to color. | *Quiero colarar.* |
| Child: | I'm missing the (crayons). | *Me faltan los creyones.* |

| Teacher: | I want to cut. | *Quiero cortar.* |
| Child: | I'm missing the (scissors). | *Me faltan las tijeras.* |

| Teacher: | I want to erase. | *Quiero borrar.* |
| Child: | I'm missing the (eraser). | *Me falta la goma de borrar.* |

| Teacher: | I want to sit. | *Quiero sentarme.* |
| Child: | I'm missing the (desk). | *Me falta el escritorio.* |

RHYME

uno, dos . . . los alumnos
tres, cuatro . . . el maestro
cinco, seis . . . los lápices
siete, ocho . . . el cuaderno
nueve, diez . . . los papeles

ADD-ON CHANT

I have, I have scissors.   *Tengo, tengo tijeras.*

pencils
papers
chalk
crayons
books, etc.

THE BOX

Place objects in box.
Direct child to:
   Open the box, find particular object, close box, and bring object to you.

Abra la caja. Encuentre el lápiz. Cierre la caja. Tráigame el lápiz.

BENDING MAN

I am cutting
   cutting,
     cutting a lot.
I begin to tire (2X)

But all I can do is
   cut,
   cut,
   cut.

I am cutting
   cutting,
     cutting a lot.

Estoy cortando,
   cortando,
     cortando mucho.
Empiezo a cansar (2X)

Pero todo lo que hago es
   cortar,
   cortar,
   cortar.

Estoy cortando,
   cortando,
     cortando mucho.

Substitute:
To write, to count, to erase, to read, to listen, to draw.

CHANT

Teacher writes the second line of each verse on the chalkboard.
She models verbs.
Children read key words, chant and perform.

In the class, in the class
I listen to the teacher,
Yes I listen.

In the class, in the class
I write my name,
Yes I write.

In the class, in the class
I read the book,
Yes I read.

In the class, in the class
I draw a design,
Yes I draw.

In the class, in the class
I erase the chalkboard,
Yes I erase.

In the class, in the class
I eat my lunch,
Yes I eat.

In the class, in the class
I greet my friends,
Yes I greet.

En la clase, en la clase
Escucho la maestra,
Escucho sí.

En la clase, en la clase
Escribo mi nombre,
Escribo sí.

En la clase, en la clase
Leo el libro,
Leo sí.

En la clase, en la clase
Dibujo un diseño,
Dibujo sí.

En la clase, en la clase
Borro la pizarra
Borro sí.

En la clase, en la clase
Como mi almuerzo,
Como sí.

En la clase, en la clase
Saludo a mis amigos,
Saludo sí.

CLASSROOM FLOOR PLAN

house vocabulary
location vocabulary

Ditto of a large square classroom.
On the bottom part print the word "red" in the target language.
On the top part print the word "green" in the target language.
On the left side print the word "yellow" in the target language.
On the right side print the word "blue" in the target language.

Teacher dictates the following.
Children draw classroom objects.

This is a classroom.
In the middle of the classroom are the desks. Draw the desks.

Touch the part that says red.
In the middle of the red part draw the teacher's desk.
To the right of the desk is the flag and the piano. Draw the flag and piano.

To the left of the desk is the closet and lunches. Draw the closet and the lunches.

Touch the part that says yellow.
In the middle of the yellow part is a chalkboard. Draw the chalkboard.
To the left of the chalkboard are books. Draw the books.
To the right of the chalkboard are the maps. Draw one map.

Touch the part that says green.
In the middle of the green part draw a door. This door goes outside.
To the right of the door is the bathroom. Draw a door and write "boys" on the door.

Touch the part that says blue.
In the middle of the blue part draw a chalkboard.
To the left of the chalkboard is Science. Draw a sink and a long table.

To the right of the chalkboard is Math. Draw three rulers.

Do you like the classroom?

Esta es la clase.
En el medio de la clase están los escritorios. Dibujen los escritorios.

Toquen la parte que dice —rojo.—
En el medio de la parte roja dibujen el escritorio de la maestra.
A la derecha del escritorio de la maestra están la bandera y el piano. Dibujen la bandera y el piano.
A la izquierda del escritorio de la maestra están el ropero y los almuerzos. Dibujen los almuerzos y el ropero.

Toquen la parte que dice —amarillo.—
En el medio de la parte amarilla está la pizarra. Dibujen la pizarra.
A la izquierda de la pizarra están los libros. Dibujen los libros.
A la derecha de la pizarra están los mapas. Dibujen el mapa.

Toquen la parte que dice —verde.—
En el medio de la parte verde dibujen la puerta. Esta puerta va afuera.
A la derecha de la puerta está el baño. Dibujen una puerta y escriben — chicos— en la puerta.

Toquen la parte que dice —azul.—
En el medio de la parte azul dibujen la pizarra.
A la izquierda de la pizarra está las ciencias. Dibujen el lavabo y una mesa larga.
A la derecha de la pizarra están las matemáticas. Dibujen tres reglas.

¿Les gusta la clase?

CHALKBOARD

Place objects along chalkboard ledge and direct child to bring you a particular
item, i.e., Bring me the chalk.   *Tráigame la tiza.*

Then have the child draw the classroom object on the board.

LISTEN AND PERFORM

Teacher models activities.

Here is the chalk.	*Aquí está la tiza.*
Here is the chalkboard.	*Aquí está la pizarra.*
Touch the chalk.	*Toque la tiza.*
Point to the chalk.	*Apunte a la tiza.*
Take the chalk.	*Tome la tiza.*
Walk to the chalkboard.	*Camine a la pizarra.*
Touch the chalkboard.	*Toque la pizarra.*
Draw a boy on the chalkboard.	*Dibuje un muchacho en la pizarra.*
Walk to your desk.	*Camine al escritorio.*
Touch your desk.	*Toque el escritorio.*
Sit down in your desk.	*Siéntese en el escritorio.*
Here is the paper.	*Aquí está el papel.*
Here is a pencil.	*Aquí está el lápiz.*
Touch the paper.	*Toque el papel.*
Point to the pencil.	*Apunte al lápiz.*
Take the pencil and touch the paper.	*Tome el lápiz y toque el papel.*
Take the pencil.	*Tome el lápiz.*
Write your name on the paper.	*Escribe su nombre en el papel.*
Like this.	*Así.*
Say your name.	*Diga su nombre.*
Point to your name.	*Apunte a su nombre.*
Erase your name.	*Borre su nombre.*
Here are the flashcards.	*Aquí están las tarjetas.*
Here are flashcards of numbers.	*Aquí están las tarjetas de números.*
Point to the flashcard.	*Apunte a la tarjeta.*
Touch the flashcard.	*Toque la tarjeta.*
Point to the number.	*Apunte al número.*
Count the number.	*Cuente el número.*
Tell me the number.	*Dígame el número.*
Write the number on the blackboard.	*Escriba el numero en la pizarra.*
Erase the number.	*Borre el número.*
Here is a book.	*Aquí está un libro.*
Open the book.	*Abra el libro.*
Show me page number 21.	*Eséñeme la página número 21.*
Read page number 21.	*Lea página número 21.*
Close the book.	*Cierre el libro.*
Put the book in your desk.	*Ponga el libro en el escritorio.*

Here are scissors.	*Aquí están las tijeras.*
Paper.	*El papel.*
And a pencil.	*Y el lápiz.*
Touch the paper.	*Toque el papel.*
Take the pencil.	*Tome el lápiz.*
Draw a girl on the paper with the pencil.	*Dibuje una muchacha en el papel con el lápiz.*
Touch the scissors.	*Toque las tijeras.*
Take the scissors.	*Tome las tijeras.*
Cut the girl.	*Corte la muchacha.*
Poor girl!	*¡Pobrecita!*

TIME

1 o'clock	*Es la una*	half hour:	*y media*
2 o'clock	*Son las dos*	quarter hour:	*y cuarto*
3 o'clock	*Son las tres*		*menos cuarto*
4 o'clock	*Son las cuartro*		
5 o'clock	*Son las cinco*		
6 o'clock	*Son las seis*		
7 o'clock	*Son las siete*		
8 o'clock	*Son las ocho*		
9 o'clock	*Son las nueve*		
10 o'clock	*Son las diez*		
11 o'clock	*Son las once*		
12 o'clock	*Son las doce*		

WHAT TIME IS IT?   *¿Qué hora es?*

hole puncher
paper plates
metal fasteners
pre-cut arrows
pencils

Take the plate.	*Tomen el plato.*
Write the numbers 1-12.	*Escriben los números uno hasta doce.*
Like this.	*Así.*
Take the pencil.	*Tomen el lápiz.*
Push it through. Like this.	*Empújenlo. Así.*
Take the arrows.	*Tomen las flechas.*
Punch a hole. Like this.	*Abren un agujero. Así.*
Attach the arrows. Like this.	*Junten las flechas. Así.*

Teacher dictates time.
Children manipulate paper clocks in seats.

Use ditto of time clocks.
Children point and identify.

Use clock stamp pad.
Children identify and label time.

BODY CLOCKS

Children use bodies to form different times.
Children may use arms while standing.

MEALTIMES

Breakfast	*el desayuno*
Lunch	*el almuerzo*
Dinner	*la cena*

See "The Menu" under Foods.
Discuss what Spanish speaking people eat for each meal.
Introduce tea time or —*la merienda.*—

12 O'CLOCK ROCK

Use cards from "Greetings and Identity" to illustrate midnight and noon.
Give the children an example:

I go to sleep at midnight.	*medianoche*
I eat lunch at noon.	*mediodía*
I get up in the morning.	*por la mañana*

CLOCK BOOKS

6 dittos
pencils
stapler

Teacher draws face of a large alarm clock, approximately 7" in diameter with a 1" base, on first ditto.
Teacher draws smaller face of clock on additional dittos with a short sentence about the time of day.

The first ditto makes the cover of the book.
Additional dittos make body of book.
Cut books out in shape of alarm clock.
Staple.

Ditto 1: Face of large alarm clock.

Ditto 2: Smaller face of clock.
　　　　Space for drawing underneath clock. Sentence:

I get up at _____ .　　　　*Me levanto a las* _____ .

Ditto 3: Smaller face of clock. Sentence:
I eat breakfast at _____ .　　　*Me desayuno a las* _____ .

Ditto 4: Smaller face of clock. Sentence:
I eat lunch at _____ .　　　　*Me almuerzo a las* _____ .

Ditto 5: Smaller face of clock. Sentence:
I eat dinner at _____ .　　　　*Me ceno a las* _____ .

Ditto 6: Smaller face of clock. Sentence:
I go to sleep at _____ .　　　*Me duermo a las* _____ .

Children put hands on each clock, write corresponding time in blank and draw appropriate picture.
Children draw a picture of themselves getting up, their favorite meals, and a bed with them in it.

CALENDAR/WEATHER

Days of the Week		**Months of the Year**		**Weather**	
Monday	*el lunes*	January	*enero*	It's sunny.	*Hace sol.*
Tuesday	*el martes*	February	*febrero*	It's hot.	*Hace calor.*
Wednesday	*el miércoles*	March	*marzo*	It's cold.	*Hace frío.*
Thursday	*el jueves*	April	*abril*	It's windy.	*Hace viento.*
Friday	*el viernes*	May	*mayo*	It's cool.	*Hace fresco.*
Saturday	*el sábado*	June	*junio*	It's snowing.	*Está nevando.*
Sunday	*el domingo*	July	*julio*	It's raining.	*Está lloviendo.*
		August	*agosto*		
		September	*septiembre*		
		October	*octubre*		
		November	*noviembre*		
		December	*diciembre*		

WINDSHIELD WIPERS

Children use hands as windshield wipers.
They chant the following:

Monday and Tuesday	*lunes y martes*
Wednesday and Thursday	*miércoles y jueves*
Friday and Saturday	*viernes y sábado*
Sunday the week.	*domingo la semana.*

BULLETIN BOARD

Use small home bulletin board for calendar.
Make individual laminated cards with holes punched at top.
Hang cards on bulletin board with tacks.

Cards include weekdays, months of year and dates.
Dates have written number word underneath.
Cards can be manipulated for every month of the year.

Make the following shape for teaching:

Today is
Yesterday was
Tomorrow is

CARDBOARD CALENDAR

one empty calendar
corresponding cards

Cardboard calendar is used for small group or individual practice.
Children sort Spanish days of week, month and written number dates for that
particular month.

HOMEMADE CALENDAR

calendar and weather vocabulary

Children make their own calendars.
The month, weekdays, dates and weather pictures are completed by the child.
The calendar is then a point of reference for questions such as:

When did it rain?	*¿Cuándo llovió?*
What day is May 14th?	*¿Qué día es el catorce de mayo?*
Point to Saturday, May 5th.	*Apunte al sábado, el cinco de mayo.*
How many sunny days were there in May?	*¿Cuántos días de sol habían en mayo?*

ADD-ON

Teacher begins with a day.
Children add on.

Today is Sunday.	*Hoy es domingo.*
It's not Sunday. It's Monday.	*No es domingo. Es lunes.*
It's not Monday. It's Tuesday.	*No es lunes. Es martes.*

Stop when you arrive at correct day.

Variation:

It is January.	*Estamos en enero.*
It's not January. It's February.	*No estamos en enero. Estamos en febrero.*
It's not February. It's March.	*No estamos en febrero. Estamos en marzo.*

BEFORE/AFTER   *antes de/después de*

Teacher makes true and false statements.
Children respond with yes or no.

January comes before February.	*Enero viene antes de febrero.*
March comes after April.	*Marzo viene después de abril.*
September comes before October.	*Septiembre viene antes de octubre.*
October comes after September.	*Octubre viene después de septiembre.*
July comes before June.	*Julio viene antes de junio.*

Teacher asks following questions.
Children answer.

Monday comes before _____ .	*El lunes viene antes del _____ .*
Wednesday comes before _____ .	*El miércoles viene antes del _____ .*
What days are class days?	*¿Qué días son días de clase?*
What days are the end of the week?	*¿Qué días son días de semana?*

127

HOLIDAYS

What month is it?	*¿En qué mes estamos?*
Columbus Day	*El día de la raza.*
All Soul's Day	*El día de los muertos.*
Christmas	*La Navidad.*
Feast of Three Kings	*El día de los tres reyes.*
Valentine's Day	*El día de los amantes.*
Easter	*La Pascua.*
Mother's Day	*El día de la madre.*
Father's Day	*El día del padre.*
Fourth of July	*El día de la independencia de América.*

BIRTHDAY DANCE
(All Around The Mulberry Bush tune)

Children stand in a circle.
Those children who have a birthday in the month called, step into the middle and make three deep bows/curtsies.
When the refrain is sung the children celebrating birthdays dance.
The remaining children clap in time.

Those who have a birthday in January,	*Los que cumplen en enero,*
January,	*enero,*
January,	*enero,*
Those who have a birthday in January,	*Los que cumplen en enero,*
Step inside.	*Pasen adentro.*
Now in the circle hold hands,	*Ya en el círculo agárrense las manos,*
hold hands,	*agárrense las manos,*
hold hands,	*agárrense las manos,*
Now in the circle hold hands,	*Ya en el círculo agárrense las manos,*
And march all around.	*Y marchen alrededor.*

Refrain:

Little boys/girls turn around,	*Muchachitos/as den la vuelta,*
turn around,	*den la vuelta,*
turn around,	*den la vuelta,*
Little boys/girls turn around,	*Muchachitos/as den la vuelta,*
Bravo! Bravo! Bravo!	*¡Bravo! ¡Bravo! ¡Bravo!*

QUERY

Teacher leads.
Children respond.

In what months do I use boots?	*¿En qué meses uso las botas?*
In what months do I use a sweater?	*¿En qué meses uso el suéter?*
In what months do I use a bathing suit?	*¿En qué meses uso el traje de baño?*
In what months do I use an umbrella?	*¿En qué meses uso el paraguas?*

LOST/FOUND

classroom objects
to lose/to find   *perder/encontrar*

Teacher gives a classroom object to five different children.
She then says: On Monday I lost my pencil.
The child holding the pencil says: I found the pencil.
Teacher says: What luck! and collects the object from the child.
She then continues with the next day of the week until all the objects have been
    collected.

On Monday I lost my pencil.	*El lunes perdí mi lápiz.*
I found the pencil.	*Encontré el lápiz.*
What luck!	*¡Qué suerte!*

Continue:

On Tuesday I lost my paper.	*El martes perdí mi papel.*
On Wednesday I lost my crayons.	*El miércoles perdí mis creyones.*
On Thursday I lost my notebook.	*El jueves perdí mi cuaderno.*
On Friday I lost my book.	*El viernes perdí mi libro.*

WEATHER CARDS

Large weather cards with an oval cut out in the center are used.
Cards can be 12" x 6" square.
The oval in the center of the square should be at least 6" x 7".
Felt pieces can be applied for colorful and durable effect.
Cover with contact paper.

Child is selected to hold a particular weather card.
Teacher hands it to the child so that he cannot see the front of the card.
The child inserts his face into the oval.
The other children give clues as to what weather card the child is holding.
The child identifies his weather card from the clues given.

Clues:

windy — blowing hard
sunny — hands over head to form an arch.
raining — fingers moving up and down.
snowing — hands holding body and shivering.
cloudy — hand held flat over head moving back and forth.

CHALKBOARD

Teacher dictates weather for each city.
Child draws weather on board.

In Buenos Aires it is sunny.	*En Buenos Aires hace sol.*
In Bogotá it is raining.	*En Bogotá está lloviendo.*
In Madrid it is cloudy.	*En Madrid está nublado.*
In Chile it is snowing.	*En Chile está nevando.*
In San Juan it is cloudy.	*En San Juan está nublado.*
In Los Angeles it is sunny.	*En Los Angeles hace sol.*
In Chicago it is snowing.	*En Chicago está nevando.*

129

DITTO

Make a ditto of the following pictures.
Have children identify the month for each picture.

January	three kings, calendar of new year	*los tres Reyes*
February	hearts	*los corazones*
March	rabbit	*el conejo*
April	rain	*la lluvia*
May	flowers	*las flores*
June	Dad with tie	*papá con corbata*
July	fireworks	*fuegos artificiales*
August	lake with boat	*el lago con bote*
September	school house	*la escuela*
October	pumpkin	*la calabaza*
November	turkey	*el pavo*
December	Christmas tree	*el árbol de Navidad*

CLOTHING

clothing or pictures of: bathing suit, shorts, jacket, mittens, boots and umbrella
weather cards

Clothing or picture cards are displayed on the floor.
Teacher holds up a particular weather card and says the following:

If it's sunny touch the bathing suit.	*Si hace sol toque el traje de baño.*
If it's hot touch the shorts.	*Si hace calor toque los pantalones cortos.*
If it's cool touch the jacket.	*Si hace fresco toque la chaqueta.*
If it's cold touch the mittens.	*Si hace frío toque los mitónes.*
If it's snowing touch the boots.	*Si nieva toque las botas.*
If it's raining touch the umbrella.	*Si llueve toque el paraguas.*

The teacher might include inappropriate matches.
In this case, the child responds, "No."

WHAT'S THE WEATHER LIKE?

clothing

Teacher begins:
I need (an umbrella).	*Necesito (el paraguas).*
What's the weather?	*¿Qué tiempo hace?*
Child responds:	
It is raining.	*Está lloviendo.*

Continue:
boots/snowing
bathing suit/it's hot
sweater/it's cool

Variation:

Teacher:
What's the weather like in December?	*Qué tiempo hace en diciembre?*
Child:	
It's cold.	*Hace frío.*

Continue with other months.

READ

The Snowy Day by Jack Ezra Keats.
An easy story to tell in Spanish. Reviews clothing and weather.

ADD-ON

weather pictures

Teacher begins.
Children add-on a weather word or picture.

It is sunny.	*Hace sol.*
It's not sunny. It's cold.	*No hace sol. Hace frío.*
It's not cold. It's hot.	*No hace frío. Hace calor.*
It's not hot. It's cool.	*No hace calor. Hace fresco.*
It's not cool. It's windy.	*No hace fresco. Hace viento.*
It's not windy. It's raining.	*No hace viento. Está lloviendo.*
It's not raining. It's snowing.	*No está lloviendo. Está nevando.*
It's not snowing. It's cloudy.	*No está nevando. Está nublado.*

SEASONS/SPORTS

Winter	*El Invierno*
hockey	*el hockey*
skating	*la patinaje*
skiing	*el esquiar*

Spring	*La Primavera*
golf	*el golf*
baseball	*el beísbol*
basketball	*el basquetbol*

Summer	*El Verano*
tennis	*el tenis*
fishing	*la pesca*
swim	*la natación*

Fall	*El Otoño*
football	*el fútbol*

SHOW ME

Teacher:
Show me baseball.   *Enseñeme el beísbol.*
Child: Child pantomimes hitting a ball.

Continue with other sports.

LIKES

Which sport do you like more: golf   *¿Qué deporte le gusta más? el golf o*
or baseball?   *el beísbol?*
    football or boxing
    skiing or skating
    tennis or swimming
    fishing or basketball

ADD-ON

Teacher begins with a sport.
Each child adds a sport.

Variation:
I like to skate.   *Me gusta patinar.*
I like to skate and play tennis.   *Me gusta patinar y jugar el tenis.*

Substitute:

play basketball	*jugar el basquetbol*
play golf	*jugar el golf*
play baseball	*jugar el beísbol*
play football	*jugar el fútbol*
to swim	*nadar*
to walk	*caminar*
to ski	*esquiar*
to fish	*pescar*
to box	*boxear*
to horseback ride	*montar a caballo*

SONG

(Farmer In The Dell tune)

I like to skate, I like to skate, In the winter I like to skate.	*Me gusta patinar,* *Me gusta patinar,* *En el invierno* *Me gusta patinar.*
I like to run, I like to run, In the spring I like to run.	*Me gusta correr,* *Me gusta correr,* *En la primavera* *Me gusta correr.*
I like to swim, I like to swim, In the summer I like to swim.	*Me gusta nadar,* *Me gusta nadar,* *En el verano* *Me gusta nadar.*
I like to read, I like to read, In the fall I like to read.	*Me gusta leer,* *Me gusta leer,* *En el otoño* *Me gusta leer.*

CHANT

Mary and Tom are swimming in
the pool,
    swimming in the pool,
    swimming in the pool,
Mary and Tom are swimming in
the pool,
And all the others want to swim.

María y Tomás están nadando en
la piscina,
    están nadando en la piscina,
    están nadando en la piscina,
María y Tomás están nadando en
la piscina,
Y todos los demás quieren nadar.

Continue:

fishing in the lake	*pescando en el lago*
skating on the ice	*patinando en el hielo*
skiing in the snow	*esquiando en la nieve*
walking in the country	*caminando en el campo*

BODY PARTS

Incorporate the use of body parts to teach sports.
Use the verb —*se usa*— or "to use."

Teacher:
What body parts are used to play
tennis?

¿Qué partes del cuerpo se usan para
jugar el tenis?

Child:
The hands, arms and legs are used.

Se usan las manos, los brazos y las
piernas.

Continue with other sports.

DRAW

Children fold white paper into four parts.
They then draw seasons and label them.

SEASON WHEEL

contact paper
construction paper
magic marker
posterboard
magazines

Cut a circle 7″ in diameter out of posterboard.
Cut four colored pies to the whole out of construction paper, i.e.
    Green — Spring
    Blue — Summer
    Orange — Autumn
    White — Winter
Glue pie pieces to the cardboard circle and label seasons.
Write out the months of the year on construction paper which is color coded for
    the season.
Cut out scenery pictures from magazines.
Mount them on construction paper which is color coded for the season.
Protect all materials with contact paper.

Child points to season picture and identifies it.
Child sorts months and places them on wheel.

BALL TOSS

4 players
1 ball
4 season cards

One season card is placed on the floor in front of each player.
Players state their seasons.
While tossing a ball, the child names the season of the catcher receiving the ball.
The catcher states his season and tosses the ball to another child while addressing
    the new season.
Once the players have memorized their seasons, the cards are turned over.
The game now proceeds from memory.
Every fourth turn the players switch positions, learn a new season, turn over their
    cards and play from memory.

SEASON CARDS

Teacher makes the following season cards:

Spring — flowers, umbrella, rain (3 cards)
Summer — lake, boat, sun (3 cards)
Autumn — pumpkin, sweater, leaves (3 cards)
Winter — boots, snow, skates, Christmas tree (4 cards)

Display three cards.
Children guess the season.

FIND THE IMPOSTER   *¿Qué está mal?*

pictures of the following:

Spring	**Summer**	**Autumn**	**Winter**
flowers	lake	leaves	snow
rain	boat	pumpkin	boots
umbrella	sun	candy	skates
pumpkin	boots	bathing suit	flowers

SONG
(Farmer In The Dell tune)

weather vocabulary

The rain in spring,	*La lluvia en la primavera,*
The rain in spring,	*La lluvia en la primavera,*
Look, feel!	*¡Miren, sientan!*
The rain in spring.	*La lluvia en la primavera.*

Continue:

The sun in summer,	*El sol en el verano,*
The sun in summer,	*El sol en el verano,*
Look, feel!	*¡Miren, sientan!*
The sun in summer.	*El sol en el verano.*
The wind in fall,	*El viento en el otoño,*
The wind in fall,	*El viento en el otoño,*
Look, feel!	*¡Miren, sientan!*
The wind in fall.	*El viento en el otoño.*
The snow in winter,	*La nieve en el invierno,*
The snow in winter,	*La nieve en el invierno,*
Look, feel!	*¡Miren, sientan!*
The snow in winter.	*La nieve en el invierno.*

CLOTHING

4 picture cards of an umbrella, bathing suit, sweater, boots

In the spring one uses _____ . *En la primavera se usa* _____ .

Continue: summer, winter, fall

QUERY

clothing pictures of: shorts, bathing suit, sweater and boots

Teacher:
What do you wear in the summer?   *¿Qué lleva en el verano?*

Child chooses picture card and completes sentence.
I wear a bathing suit.   *Llevo el traje de baño.*

ANIMALS

season cards
pictures of: fish, birds, squirrels, deer

Introduce the concept of "are found in" or *—se encuentra/n.—*
Teacher places animal picture on appropriate season card and says:

Fish are found in the summer.	*Se encuentra el pescado en el verano.*
Birds are found in the spring.	*Se encuentran los pájaros en la primavera.*
Squirrels are found in the fall.	*Se encuentran las ardillas en el otoño.*
Deer are found in the winter.	*Se encuentra el ciervo en el invierno.*

ORDINAL NUMBERS   *primero, segundo, tercero, cuarto*

season pictures

Teacher demonstrates ordinal number progression using season pictures.
She then asks:
What season comes first?   *¿Qué estación viene primero?*
Child provides teacher with appropriate season card and identifies the season.

READ

Spring, Summer, Fall, Winter from Barron's Educational Series.
Beautifully illustrated books and easy to read.

LISTEN AND PERFORM

clothing, house and weather vocabulary
season pictures
props: Spring — jacket, purse, flowers
       Summer — bathing suit, towel
       Fall — sweater, pants, leaves
       Winter — overcoat, hat, mittens, scarf, boots

Teacher models.
Child imitates.

Variation:

Turn on Baroque music (Handel, Bach).
Pass out this lesson.
Older children read the imagery silently.

SPRING

It is spring and it is sunny.
Go to the window.
Listen.
The birds are singing.
Put on your jacket.
Take a bag.
Walk to the door.
Go outside.
Look at the flowers! How beautiful
they are!
Pick three flowers for your mom.
Put them in your bag.

SUMMER

It is summer and it is hot.
Go to the window.
Look.
The children are swimming in the lake.
Put on your bathing suit.
Bring a towel.
Walk to the door.
Go outside.
Run to the lake.
Jump in the lake.
Swim.

AUTUMN

It is autumn and it is cool.
Go to the window.
It's windy. Blow like the wind.
The leaves are falling.
Put on your sweater.
Put on your pants.
Walk to the door.
Go outside.
Greet your friends.
Now play in the leaves.

WINTER

It is winter and it is cold.
Go to the window.
It is snowing. Taste the snow.
Put on your coat.
Put on your hat.
Put on your mittens.
Put on your scarf.
Put on your boots.
Go to the door.
Go outside.
Walk in the snow.

La Primavera

Es primavera y hace sol.
Vaya a la ventana.
Escuche.
Los pájaros están cantando.
Póngase la chaqueta.
Tome la bolsa.
Camine a la puerta.
Vaya afuera.

Mire las flores. ¡Qué hermosas son!
Coja tres flores para su mamá.
Póngalas en su bolsa.

El Verano

Es verano y hace calor.
Vaya a la ventana.
Mire.
Los niños están nadando en el lago.
Póngase el traje de baño.
Traiga una toalla.
Camine a la puerta.
Vaya afuera.
Corre al lago.
Salte en el lago.
Nade.

El Otoño

Es otoño y hace fresco.
Vaya a la ventana.
Hace viento. Sople como el viento.
Las hojas están cayendo.
Póngase el suéter.
Póngase los pantalones.
Camine a la puerta.
Vaya afuera.
Salude a sus amigos.
Ahora juegue en las hojas.

El Invierno

Es invierno y hace frío.
Vaya a la ventana.
Está nevando. Pruebe la nieve.
Póngase el abrigo.
Póngase el sombrero.
Póngase los mitónes.
Póngase la bufanda.
Póngase las botas.
Vaya a la puerta.
Vaya afuera.
Camine en la nieve.

THE COMMUNITY

grocery store	*la tienda de comestibles*
school	*la escuela*
library	*la biblioteca*
church	*la iglesia*
bank	*el banco*
hospital	*el hospital*
movie theatre	*el cine*
restaurant	*el restaurante*
post office	*el correo*
pharmacy	*la farmacia*
bakery	*la panadería*
butcher shop	*la carnicería*
candy store	*la confitería*
dentist	*la dentista*
shoe store	*la zapatería*
police	*la policía*
park	*el parque*
hairdresser	*la peluquería*
ice cream parlor	*la heladería*
clothing store	*la ropería*
city	*la ciudad*
farm	*la granja*
beach	*la playa*
park	*el parque*
lake	*el lago*

WHERE YA GOIN'?

Ad-on activity.
Teacher asks each child:

Where ya goin'?	*¿Adónde va?*
Child responds:	
I'm going to school.	*Voy a la escuela.*
Next child:	
I'm going to the movies.	*Voy al cine.*

CHALKBOARD

Teacher introduces analogies through chalkboard pictures.
She first draws several buildings.
The teacher says:

This is a building.	*Este es un edificio.*
Inside the building is (bread).	*Dentro del edificio está (el pan).*
The building is called a (bakery).	*El edificio se llama (la panadería).*

She continues with each area of the community.
The teacher may draw tall, short, big or small buildings.
Later, the class discusses how many buildings there are, their size and shape.

Variation:
Teacher draws buildings on the chalkboard as illustrated above.
Children receive building counterparts, i.e. money, candy, book, stamp, blouse, shoe.
Teacher then says the following:

If you have the bread, go to the bakery.   *Si tiene el pan, vaya a la panadería.*
Child then stands next to the bakery building on the board.
Continue with other stores.

shoe store
candy store
bank
post office
library
clothing store

SONG
(Farmer In The Dell tune)

The bread in the bakery,	*El pan en la panadería,*
The bread in the bakery,	*El pan en la panadería,*
Look! See!	*¡Miren! ¡Vean!*
The bread in the bakery.	*El pan en la panadería.*
meat/butcher shop	*la carne/la carnicería*
stamps/post office	*las estampillas/el correo*
food/grocery store	*la comida/la tienda*
drugs/pharmacy	*las medicinas/la farmacia*
money/bank	*el dinero/el banco*
candy/candy store	*los dulces/la confitería*
books/library	*los libros/la biblioteca*
Jesus/church	*Jesus/la iglesia*
the sick/hospital	*los enfermos/el hospital*
movies/theatre	*las peliculas/el cine*

CLOTHING

pants   school
dress   church
bathing suit   beach
purse   movies

Teacher draws clothing and places in the community on the blackboard.
She begins each sentence and points to a place.
Child completes the sentence and points to an article of clothing.

Teacher:
When I go to school I wear . . .   *Cuando voy a la escuela llevo . . .*
Child:
I wear pants.   *Llevo los pantalones.*

Continue:
When I go to church/I wear a dress.
When I go to the beach/I wear a bathing suit.
When I go to the movies/I carry a purse.

139

ERRANDS

Cards:

Teacher cuts 8-1/2″ x 11″ paper or tagboard in half.
On one half she draws a house with a loaf of bread in it.
On the other half she draws just the loaf of bread.
The teacher then labels each half in the target language, i.e. bakery/bread.

Game:

Divide the class into two teams facing each other.
Give one team picture cards, i.e. bread, candy, food.
Give the other team places in the community, i.e. bakery, candy store, grocery store.

The first team member having the bread card says:
I need bread.   Necesito pan.
The opposing team member, having the bakery card, says:
I go to the bakery.   Voy a la panadería.

Continue:

meat/butcher's shop	books/library
stamps/post office	Jesus/church
food/store	doctor/hospital
drugs/pharmacy	shoes/shoe store
money/bank	teeth/dentist
candy/candy store	ice cream/ice cream parlor

THE HOUSE

See: The House under "Animals" and "House."

Teacher uses community cards and their counterparts to illustrate the following sentences.
Children draw and label corresponding pictures on each page of their "house" books.

1. The post office is a house for letters.   El correo es una casa para cartas.
2. The supermarket is a house for food.   (comida)
3. The pharmacy is a house for medicines.   (medicinas)
4. The bank is a house for money.   (dinero)
5. The candy store is a house for candy.   (dulces)
6. The library is a house for books.   (libros)
7. The church is a house for Jesus.   (Jesús)
8. The hospital is a house for the sick.   (los enfermos)
9. The school is a house for students.   (alumnos)
10. The movie theatre is a house for movies.   (películas)

SITUATIONS

Teacher sets up six stations in the classroom.
They are: library, restaurant, bank, store, post office and dentist's office.
She models each sentence and says what she is doing.
Child volunteer then follows her commands.

LIBRARY: (Little Red Riding Hood book, 3 x 5 card, pencil)

Go to the library.	*Vaya a la biblioteca.*
Take the book called, Little Red Riding Hood.	*Tome el libro que se llama, Caperucita Roja.*
Open the book.	*Abra el libro.*
Take the card.	*Tome la tarjeta.*
Write your name on the card.	*Escriba su nombre en la tarjeta.*

RESTAURANT: (menu, feeling card)

Go to the restaurant.	*Vaya al restaurante.*
Show me the card, I am hungry.	*Enséñeme la tarjeta, tengo hambre.*
Take the menu.	*Tome el menú.*
Open the menu.	*Abra el menú.*
Ask for a hamburger, french fries and a coke.	*Pida una hamburguesa, papas fritas y coca cola.*
Tell the waiter, thank you.	*Dígale al mozo, Gracias.*

BANK: (money, purse)

Go to the bank.	*Vaya al banco.*
Point to the money.	*Apunte al dinero.*
Take the purse.	*Tome la bolsa.*
Ask for $50.00	*Pida cincuenta dólares.*
Count $50.00	*Cuente cincuenta dólares.*
Put the money in the purse.	*Ponga el dinero en la bolsa.*

STORE: (blouse, money)

Go to the clothing store.	*Vaya a la ropería.*
Put on the blouse.	*Póngase la blusa.*
Take off the blouse.	*Quítese la blusa.*
Buy the blouse.	*Compre la blusa.*
The blouse costs $25.00.	*La blusa cuesta veinticinco dólares.*
Count to 25.	*Cuente hasta veinticinco.*
Pay the man.	*Pague el señor.*

POST OFFICE: (stamps, purse, letters, mailbox)

Go to the post office.	*Vaya al correo.*
Take the stamps.	*Tome las estampillas.*
Take the purse.	*Tome la bolsa.*
Open the purse.	*Abra la bolsa.*
Take out two letters from the purse.	*Saque dos cartas de la bolsa.*
Put the stamps on the letters.	*Ponga las estampillas en las cartas.*
Mail the letters.	*Envíe las cartas.*

DENTIST: (chair)

Go to the dentist.	*Vaya al dentista.*
Your tooth hurts.	*Le duele el diente.*
Open your mouth.	*Abra la boca.*
Touch the tooth that hurts.	*Toque el diente que le duele.*
Close your mouth.	*Cierre la boca.*
Sit down in the chair.	*Siéntese en la silla.*

PROFESSIONS

mother	*la madre*
teacher	*la maestra*
nurse	*la enfermera*
doctor	*el doctor*
policeman	*el policía*
fireman	*el bombero*
dentist	*el dentista*
chef	*el cocinero*
farmer	*el granjero*
priest	*el sacerdote*

SONG
(Did You Ever See a Lassie tune)

Teacher passes out occupation flashcards.

Who is the fireman,
    the fireman,
    the fireman,
Who is the fireman?
Step forward please.

¿Quién es el bombero,
    el bombero,
    el bombero,
¿Quién es el bombero?
Adelante por favor.

Substitute:
  policeman
  dentist
  teacher
  nurse

WHERE DO THEY WORK?

¿Dónde trabaja . . . ?

Correlate community with the professions.
Begin by asking a child to draw a particular building on the board.

Teacher: Draw a building.
        Draw a flag on the building.
        The building is called a school.
        The teacher works in the school.

Continue with other professions.

The doctor works in the hospital.	*El doctor trabaja en el hospital.*
The policeman works in the street.	*(la calle)*
The dentist works in the office.	*(la oficina)*
The mother works at home.	*(en casa)*
The farmer works on the farm.	*(la granja)*
The priest works at the church.	*(la iglesia)*
The chef works in the restaurant.	*(el restaurante)*
The fireman works at the fire station.	*(la casa de bomberos)*
The teacher works in the school.	*(la escuela)*

THE BAG

paper bag
picture cards of:
   fireman's hat
   policeman's hat
   chef's hat
   a fish
   a desk with an apple on it

Each child selects a card from the bag.
When he sees the picture he identifies the profession belonging to the picture.
For example:
It's the teacher's.   *Es de la maestra.*

WHO/WHAT DO THEY TAKE CARE OF?   *Cuida de los . . .*

The doctor takes care of the sick.	*El doctor cuida de los enfermos.*
The policeman takes care of people.	*(la gente)*
The dentist takes care of teeth.	*(los dientes)*
The mother takes care of children.	*(los niños)*
The farmer takes care of animals.	*(los animales)*
The chef takes care of food.	*(la comida)*
The fireman takes care of fires.	*(los fuegos)*
The teacher takes care of students.	*(los alumnos)*

COLORS

Teacher displays flashcards of a hunter, fireman, seaman, chef and skier.
Teacher reads each description.
Children guess which profession.

Green, green, green	*Verde, verde, verde*
the clothes that I wear	*el vestido que llevo*
green, green, green	*verde, verde, verde*
are all that I have	*es todo lo que tengo*
because I like green of the forest	*porque me gusta verde del bosque*
my friend is a hunter.	*mi amigo es* **un cazador.**
Red, red, red	*Rojo, rojo, rojo*
the clothes that I wear	*el vestido que llevo*
red, red, red	*rojo, rojo, rojo*
are all that I have	*es todo lo que tengo*
because I like red of the fire	*porque me gusta rojo del fuego*
my friend is a fireman.	*mi amigo es* **un bombero.**
Blue, blue, blue	*Azul, azul, azul*
the clothes that I wear	*el vestido que llevo*
blue, blue, blue	*azul, azul, azul*
are all that I have	*es todo lo que tengo*
because I like blue of the sea	*porque me gusta azul del mar*
my friend is a seaman.	*mi amigo es* **un marino.**

Yellow, yellow, yellow
the clothes that I wear
Yellow, yellow, yellow
are all that I have
because I like yellow of the tortilla
my friend is a chef.

White, white, white
the clothes that I wear
white, white, white
are all that I have
because I like white of the snow
my friend is a skier.

Amarillo, amarillo, amarillo
el vestido que llevo
Amarillo, amarillo, amarillo
es todo lo que tengo
porque me gusta amarillo de la tortilla
*mi amigo es **un cocinero.***

Blanco, blanco, blanco
el vestido que llevo
blanco, blanco, blanco
es todo lo que tengo
porque me gusta blanco de la nieve
*mi amigo es **un esquiador.***

TRANSPORTATION

plane	*el avión*
train	*el tren*
car	*el coche*
bicycle	*la bicicleta*
boat	*el bote, el barco (ship)*
taxi	*el taxi*
motorcycle	*la motocicleta*
bus	*el ómnibus*
truck	*el camión*
helicopter	*el helicóptero*

COLORS

Draw a plane.	*Dibuje un avión.*
Color it grey.	*Píntelo gris.*

Draw a taxi. Color it yellow.
Draw a boat. Color it white.
Draw a bicycle. Color it blue.
Draw a truck. Color it red.
Draw a train. Color it brown.
Draw a car. Color it green.
Draw a motorcycle. Color it black.
Draw a bus. Color it orange.

MODES OF TRAVEL

Teacher introduces "I travel" or —*viajo.*—

by air	*por aire*
by land	*por tierra*
by sea	*por mar*

Teacher reads sentence.
Children fill in mode of transportation.
Several choices are available.

I travel by air, I am a _____ .   *Viajo por aire, soy un _____ .*
I travel by sea, I am a _____ .
I travel by land, I am a _____ .

ADD-ON

Teacher begins:
I travel by ship.   *Viajo por barco.*
Children add on a mode of transportation.
After each response the teacher says:
Bon voyage!   *¡Buen viaje!*

ARRIVES/DEPARTS   *Llega/sale*

Teacher uses chalkboard for drawing two continents and two U.S. cities.
She uses a plane to illustrate arrival and departure from two continents.
She uses a train to illustrate arrival and departure from two U.S. cities.

Teacher marks "arrives" and "departs" in the appropriate continent or city.
Teacher reads the following statements.
Child goes up to the board and records the time, in the appropriate city or continent.

The plane arrives in Australia at 6:30 p.m.   *El avión llega en Australia a las seis y*
                                               media de la tarde.
The plane leaves Europe at 8:00 a.m.
The train leaves Detroit at 4:00 p.m.
The train arrives in Chicago at 9:00 p.m.

OPPOSITES

Which is faster?   *¿Cuál transporte es más rápido?*
   the plane or the taxi
   the ship or the bicycle.

Which is slower?   *¿Cuál es más despacio?*
   the train or the bus
   the car or the helicopter.

Which is larger?   *¿Cuál es más grande?*
   the bike or the motorcycle
   the truck or the car

Which is smaller?   *¿Cuál es más pequeño?*
   the taxi or the train
   the car or the bus

LOCATION

community posterboard
directions
toy transportation

Direct the child to place (the car):
   in front of the bank
   next to the church
   to the right of the hospital
   behind the school, etc.

146

THE COMMUNITY

flashcards or toy replicas of a plane, car, boat, train, bike

Teacher draws a community on a large posterboard.
Include a park, a lake, an airport, train station, a farm, and a beach.
Read the following passages.
Include the additional buildings on your posterboard.
Instruct individual children to do the following:

Take the car.	*Tome el coche.*
Go to the grocery store.	*Vaya a la tienda.*
Go to the bank.	*Vaya al banco.*
Go to the post office.	*Vaya al correo.*
Stop at the restaurant.	*Pare al restaurante.*
Take the airplane.	*Tome el avión.*
Fly over the church.	*Vuela sobre la iglesia.*
Fly over the school.	*Vuela sobre la escuela.*
Fly over the hospital.	*Vuela sobre el hospital.*
Stop at the airport.	*Pare en el aeropuerto.*
Take the boat.	*Tome el bote.*
Travel past the house.	*Pasee por las casas.*
Travel past the park.	*Pasee por el parque.*
Travel past the island.	*Pasee por la isla.*
Stop at the beach.	*Pare en la playa.*
Take the train.	*Tome el tren.*
Travel past the farm.	*Pasee por la granja.*
Travel past the lake.	*Pasee por el lago.*
Travel past the city.	*Pasee por la ciudad.*
Stop at the station.	*Pare en la estación.*
Take the bike.	*Tome la bicicleta.*
Go to the ice cream store.	*Vaya a la heladería.*
Go to the movies.	*Vaya al cine.*
Go to the library.	*Vaya a la biblioteca.*
Go home.	*Vaya a casa.*

HOW MANY?

Teacher:
How many tires does a bicycle have?   *¿Cuántas llantas tiene la bicicleta?*
Child:
It has (2, 3,4, or more) tires.   *Tiene (dos, tres, cuatro o más) llantas.*

If it has none, —*no tiene.*—

Continue:

plane (small)	motorcycle
train	bus
car	truck (small)
boat	helicopter
taxi	

147

DESTINATION

Match the following modes of transportation with their location.

Teacher:
Where do you find a boat?   *¿Dónde se encuentra un bote?*
Child:
in the lake   *en el lago*

Continue:

bus/school   *la escuela*
plane/airport   *el aeropuerto*
train/station   *la estación*
horse/farm   *la granja*

Variation:

Teacher:
When I want to see a boat . . .   *Cuando quiero ver un bote . . .*
Child:
I go to the lake.   *Voy al lago.*

CULTURE

Culture is an important part of an early foreign language program. Children are interested in what other people eat, how they dance, what they wear and what the language sounds like in song. These interests can be captured by preparing native foods, doing art and history projects and through song and dance. The sound of the new language and these cultural experiences will stimulate the child who is trying to order his environment.

The following ideas, recipes and activities will whet the child's appetite for culture. More importantly, this new cultural awareness will be acquired effortlessly.

SHOW AND TELL

record player
music
artifacts

Turn on some native music.
Children are seated in a large circle.
Put small items like filigree jewelry, bread dough pins, natural seed necklaces, onyx stone, money or postcards on a tray and pass it around.
Children and teacher can put on native clothing and carry typical purses, belts, hats or pottery of the country.

Use show and tell time to share souvenirs, books or postcards that children bring in from trips. Acknowledging the child's contribution will make him feel important and valuable.

PICASSO

paper
crayons
construction paper
glue

Tell the children about Picasso.
Show them samples of his art.
Review colors and geometric shapes in Spanish.
Children draw and color their own Picasso masterpiece.
They may also glue pre-cut geometric shapes onto construction paper for a different effect.

BULLFIGHT

popsicle sticks
tagboard or heavy paper
glue
paper
crayons

to push	empujar
to kill	matar
vest	el chaleco
slippers	las zapatillas
sword	la espada

Create a bullfight ring by gluing popsicle sticks to a cardboard backing.
The walls of the ring are as tall as the sticks.
The ring is enclosed.

Make two smaller walls inside the ring of 6 sticks each.
An opening is between the two smaller walls.
This area is where the bull enters the ring.

Children can then draw a person.
They color the person and glue him to a stick.
These different people are the spectators.

One child is chosen to draw the bull. (el toro)
Another child is chosen to draw the bullfighter. (el torero)

The fight begins.
3 volunteers
foil sword
vest
slippers

Take the sword.	Tome la espada.
Point to the bull.	Apunte al toro.
Point to the bullfighter.	Apunte al torero.
Point to the vest.	Apunte al chaleco.
Point to the slippers.	Apunte a las zapatillas.

Look at the bull.	Mire el toro.
Touch the bull.	Toque el toro.
Push the bull.	Empuje el toro.
Kill the bull.	Mate el toro.

CASTLES   el castillo

construction paper
glue
posterboard

Use picture books of Spain to introduce castles.

Children can then build their own castle using blocks or even legos.
Teacher may wish to draw the outline of a castle on a posterboard.
The children can each paste several pre-cut brown squares and glue them on the
   castle.

DANCE   *(El Malambo)*   Argentina

drums

This is a virility dance.
Two contestants compete to see who can dance the longest time on one leg to the
  beat of the drums.

DANCE   *(El Tango)*   Argentina

handkerchiefs

Show the children some steps of the tango.
Dance cheek to cheek, arms outstretched, dancing first to the right, then to the left.
Use handkerchiefs, held over head or behind back, to illustrate the romance and
  variety of the dance.

DANCE   *(El Huayno)*   Peru

1. Partners stand a few feet apart. With skipping step (clicking heels), they come
     together, bow, and return to place.
2. Partners come together and circle around (back to back), and return to place.
3. Partners come together, hook right arms, circle, and back to place. Repeat with
     left arms.
4. Children take out handkerchiefs (girls hold handkerchief over head, boys hold
     handkerchief behind their backs).
   a. They come together, touching handkerchiefs, and return to place.
   b. Come together, hook handkerchiefs, and turn in place, first to the right, then
        to the left, they release handkerchiefs and return to place.
5. Partners come together, boy places handkerchief around girl's neck and draws
     her forward as dance ends.
The dance step is a running hop step, with clicking heels. Hand clapping in rhythm
  with the music, during the dance is optional.

DANCE   *(La Bamba)*

maracas

Children sing and wiggle while shaking maracas.

¡Para bailar la bam-ba, da-da da
Para bailar la bam-ba, da-da da
Para bailer la bam-ba, da-da da
se necesita un poco de gracia y otra cosita!

Refrain:
Bam-ba, bamba
bam-ba, bamba
bam-ba, bamba
bam-ba, bamba

Repeat 1st verse.

¡Ay arriba y arriba y arriba iré!
Yo no soy marinero, por ti seré.

Repeat Refrain.
Repeat 1st verse.

TORTA DE CIELO

From **Mexican Cookery** ©HP Books, Inc.
Tucson, AZ 85703, (602) 888-2150

Put/place	*Ponga*
Cover	*Cubra*
Remove from heat	*Quite del fuego*

The teacher can do everything up to the asterisk.
Children do the rest.
This is a wonderful recipe to make for a Parent's Night presentation.
Cut the torte into bite-size pieces for sampling.
Parents will want the recipe.
Refrigerate any remaining cake, it will taste even better the next day.

1/2 lb. unblanched almonds	*las almendras no blanqueadas*
water	*el agua*
1-1/3 cups sugar	*el azúcar*
6 eggs, separated	*los huevos*
pinch of salt	*la sal*
1 tablespoon all-purpose flour	*una cucharada de harina*
1 tablespoon dark rum	*el ron*
1/4 teaspoon cream of tartar	*la crema de tártara*
4 to 6 blanched almonds, chopped	*las almendras blanqueadas y cortadas*

*Drain/pat dry	*Seque*	egg white	*la clara*
Press	*Apriete*	Fold	*Doble*
waxed paper	*papel encerado*	Serves	*Sirva*
Grease	*Engrase*	Bake	*Cocine al horno*
Grind	*Muela*	Remove	*Quite*
paste	*la pasta*	Cut	*Corte*
Beat	*Bata*	Decorate	*Adorne*

The night before, place 1/2 pound almonds in a medium saucepan. Cover with water and bring to a boil. Remove from heat and let stand 5 minutes; drain. Press soaked almonds between your fingers to remove skins. Return skinned almonds to saucepan. Cover with cold water and let stand overnight. *Just before making torte, drain almonds and pat dry with paper towels.

Grease a 9-1/2″ springform pan. Line bottom with waxed paper. Grease paper; set pan aside.

Preheat oven to 350°F.

In blender or food processor, grind almonds with 2/3 cup sugar until very fine, almost a paste.

In a large bowl, beat egg yolks, remaining 2/3 cup sugar and salt until light and creamy. Beat in flour, then rum. Beat in almond mixture.

In a large bowl, beat egg whites with cream of tartar until stiff. Fold 1/3 of the egg whites into nut mixture, then fold in remaining egg whites lightly but thoroughly. Turn into prepared pan.

Bake 35 minutes or until browned and cake has begun to shrink from side of pan. Cake will rise as it bakes, begin to settle in the center and settle further as it cools. Cool in pan on a rack. When torte is completely cool, run a knife around edge of pan to loosen. Remove side of pan.

Cut in wedges and place on a serving plate. Decorate each wedge with a few pieces of coarsely chopped almonds. Makes 8 servings.

EMPANADAS DE QUESO

(cheese pastries)   Argentina

This is an easy and delicious recipe to prepare.
The children are particularly interested in cutting the circles out with a glass.
They like pinching the empanadas shut.
Many hands on the dough make it sticky.
Add a little flour to alleviate this problem.

1-1/2 cups flour	*la harina*
1/2 teaspoon salt	*media cucharadita de sal*
1/2 teaspoon sugar	*media cucharadita de azúcar*
1 teaspoon baking powder	*levadura en polvo*
1/2 cup butter (1 stick), cut into small pieces	*la mantequilla cortada*
3 egg yolks	*las yemas*
1/3 cup milk	*la leche*
2 egg whites	*las claras*
1-1/2 cups grated sharp cheddar cheese	*el queso rallado*
1/2 teaspoon chili powder	*polvo de chiles*

Combine	*Combine*	Add	*Añada*
Cut	*Corte*	Beat	*Bata*
Stir	*Revuelve*	Chill	*Enfrie*
Fold	*Doble*	Roll out	*Extienda*
Dough	*la masa*	Put	*Ponga*
Moisten/Press	*Moje/Apriete*	Arrange	*Arregle*
Bake	*Cocine al horno*	Makes	*Hace*

Combine the flour with the salt, sugar and baking powder in a bowl.
Add the butter and cut into the flour with a pastry blender or 2 knives.
Beat the egg yolks lightly and combine with the milk. Stir in to the flour to form a soft dough.
Wrap in waxed paper and chill for 1 hour.
Beat the egg whites and fold in the grated cheese and chili powder.
Roll out the dough **as thinly as possible** on a floured board.
Cut the dough into 48 circles with a glass.
Place 1/3 tablespoon of the cheese mixture on half of the circles and cover with the remaining circles.
Moisten the edges with a little water and press together.
Arrange the pastries on a baking sheet and bake in a preheated 375° oven for 15 minutes. Makes 20-24 servings.

ANISE COOKIES

Spain

Follow any recipe in a standard cookbook.

SPANISH SPOKEN HERE

Aquí se habla español

Paint a piece of 2' x 2' plywood white.
Draw a map of the world showing the continents.
Paint the continents blue.
Paint the countries where Spanish is spoken orange.

GEOGRAPHY

Montessori wooden map insets
envelopes
construction paper
bulletin board pins
pencils
scissors

Children trace and pin-punch the outline of a country.
They label each country and place in an envelope.
When all the pertinent countries of a continent have been cut out or pin-punched,
  they can then be glued to pages to form a book.

FLAGS

pre-cut pieces of construction paper
glue
straws
stapler
flag reference: encyclopedia, Discovery Toys atlas book

Child selects country he is going to represent.
Children glue pre-cut squares and strips together.
The national symbol is drawn on the flag.
Straws are stapled onto the flags for carrying.

Children process around the classroom.
When teacher calls the country of the flag they represent, the children shout,
  ¡Vivan los Hispanos! (Long live the Spanish!)

Children can describe the colors of their flags.
Teacher can make a graph on the board listing the countries having red in their
  flag, blue, green, etc.

CURRENCY

map or globe
ditto of North, South and Central America and Europe
flags

Children read the name of the country on the currency.
They find that country on the globe.
They record the name of the money, i.e. "peso," on the South America ditto under
  Argentina.

Children can then sort the money by country.
They lay handmade flags of countries across the floor.
The currency for each country is then placed in a column beneath the flag.

Children enjoy this activity.
Make sure you have several duplicates of money for more interesting sorting.
Pin-punched countries may be substituted for flags.

*Laminate or "contact" the currency for safekeeping.

SEARCH

globe, world map
ditto

Use the globe to find these places.
Draw the word or picture you found at each place.

tortilla	1. Mexico
quetzal bird, banana, volcano	2. Guatemala
oil	3. Venezuela
coffee, emerald	4. Colombia
sun	5. Ecuador
alpaca, gold	6. Peru
tin can, Coya Indian	7. Bolivia
copper penny	8. Chile
beef cattle	9. Argentina
oranges, olives, bull	10. Spain

RELIGION

The Catholic Church is a predominant force in Latin American life.
Small shrines are built at the side of the road where an accident has occurred.
Pilgrimages are made to a holy place for special favors.
Processions in the street are common to celebrate religious holidays.

See —el Día de los Muertos— or All Soul's Day.
See —las Posadas— or Christmas celebrations from Dec. 16 to Dec. 24.
See —la Nochebuena— or Christmas Eve.
See —la Navidad— or Christmas under "Holidays".
See —El Día de los tres reyes magos — or the feast of the three wise men.
See —la Pascua— or Easter.

NAMES

Spanish people have two family names, the family name of the father followed by the maiden name of the mother. An example might be:
Juan Lopez **y** Carranza which can be shortened to Juan Lopez. In this case the mother's family name has been omitted.

When a woman marries, she keeps her family name and adds the family name of her husband. An example is: María Gomez **de** Gonzalez.

Spanish children are usually named after a saint.
The children celebrate their saint's day.

SCHOOLS

In Latin America education is free except for private schools.
Different months, seasons. and weather characterize the school year in South America.

TRANSPORTATION

Public transportation is widely used in South America.
Taxis are common.
Many people walk.

FOOD
(See Holiday Recipes)

In South America four meals a day are served. They are:
A light breakfast, the main meal at lunch, a snack and tea in the late afternoon, and a
   late night light supper.
In Latin America both hands are above the table and used for eating.

In Argentina, table wine is served at meals with a little soda water.
Chocolate is a favorite sweet in Mexico and is served warm.
Yerba mate is a Spanish American tea. It is served in a gourd. A silver tube is used to
   strain and sip the tea.
Hispanic people enjoy fresh bread which is broken from the loaf and eaten with the
   meal.

ATTITUDES

In Mexico and other Hispanic countries the concept of time is more relaxed.
Individuals are more important than schedules.
Business contacts can be made during the "siesta" or rest time of 2-3 hours in the
   afternoon.
Hispanic peoples are very hospitable.
Gift giving is important and serenading (singing songs to loved ones) is popular.

SHOPPING

Packages and gifts are wrapped before leaving the store.
While doing errands you may find: beggars *(mendigos)* and street vendors
   (vendedores) of flowers *(flores),* magazines *(revistas),* and newspapers
   (periódicos).
The magazines and newspapers are sold in a kiosk. *(kiosco)*

CLOTHING

el sarape	A brightly colored blanket that is worn over the shoulders.
el poncho	Argentine cloak with a slit for the head.
el rebozo	A shawl worn by women.
blouses	Mexican blouses are beautifully embroidered.
hats and caps	The type, banding and color indicate a city or region much like different ponchos do in Argentina.
la faja	A sash worn by men in native garb.
las bombachas	Knickers worn by men in traditional costume.
la mantilla	A lace veil worn by women over the head in church.

MUSIC

Each country has typical songs and dances.
Common instruments and terms are:

la guitarra	the guitar
las maracas	gourds with pebbles inside which are shaken
las castañuelas	castanets
los mariachis	strolling musicians

ANIMALS

Each country has typical animals.

la llama	of South America
quetzal bird	of Guatemala
la alpaca	(llama family) of Peru
el condor	(condor eagle) of Andes Mountains

DISTANCE

Children are intrigued by how long a plane ride it is to:
   Mexico
   Peru
   Argentina
   Spain

CURRENCY

Some banks keep a reserve of foreign money on hand.
If not, you can order some.
Each country has different currency of different value.
A few are listed below.

Mexico	*peso, centavo*
Spain	*peseta*
Colombia	*peso, centavo*
Ecuador	*sucre, centavo*
Peru	*sol*
Chile	*peso, escudo*
Argentina	*peso, centavo*

SPORTS

soccer	*el fútbol*
bullfight	*corrida de toros*
cowboy	*el gaucho (Argentina)*
bullfighter	*el torero*

HOLIDAYS

If culture is defined as a style of social and artistic expression peculiar to a people, then holidays can reveal much about the people whose language the child is acquiring. With this in mind, I have selected activities to illustrate Hispanic celebrations. The activities are organized by months of the American school year.

LABOR DAY

Talk about Labor Day as being the Day of the Worker or *Día del Trabajador.*

Children fold paper into four parts and draw a policeman, a doctor, a baker, and a teacher.
Children talk about where their parents work.
Talk about the need to have money to live. Pass around currency from various Spanish speaking countries. Children read the name of the country on the money. They discover the name of the money. They read how much money they have.

Note that in other countries Labor Day is celebrated on May 1.

COLUMBUS DAY

Tell the children about *el Día de la Raza,* celebrated October 12.

This day celebrates the Spanish heritage and Christopher Columbus' arrival in America. His three ships were named *la Niña, la Pinta and the Santa María.* The King and Queen of Spain were Ferdinand and Isabella. The year of the trip was 1492.

Have the children draw a picture of this story using the following words:

Día de la Raza	*La Santa María*
La Reina Isabella	*España*
Colón	*1492*
La Niña	*12 de Octubre*
La Pinta	

Make a huge ship on posterboard.
The whole class participates by gluing yarn and cutting burlap or material for the sails.

HALLOWEEN   *El Día de las Brujas*

SONG
(Farmer In The Dell tune)

The witch in the night,	*La bruja en la noche,*
The witch in the night,	*La bruja en la noche,*
Oh, my God!	*¡Ay, Dios mío!*
The witch in the night.	*La bruja en la noche.*

Continue:

the ghost	*la fantasma*
the pumpkin	*la calabaza*
the skeleton	*el esqueleto*
the cat	*el gato*

SONG

(La Cucaracha tune)

The witch	*La bru-ja*
The witch	*La bru-ja*
I look at her with horror	*Ya la miro con horror*
because on her	*porque en ella*
because on her	*porque en ella*
there is an ugly face.	*una cara fea ya está.*
The ghost	*La fantas-ma*
The ghost	*La fantas-ma*
I look at her with fright	*Ya la miro con susto*
because on her	*porque en ella*
because on her	*porque en ella*
there are such scary eyes.	*hay unos ojos tan espantosos.*

THUMBPRINTS

number vocabulary
black construction paper
scissors
white finger paint

Teacher or children can cut out a simple shape of a tall house.
Children then make spooks in the house by dipping their thumbs into the white
    paint and making thumbprints throughout the house.
Children count how many spooks are in their house in the target language.

SMILE

Children make their own paper pumpkins repeating all the while the words for
    eyes, nose and mouth.
Then they print their Spanish name in the form of a smile.

DRAW

Children fold white paper into four parts. They draw and label a ghost, a witch, a
    pumpkin and a skeleton. Or a black cat, a vampire, a skeleton, and a spider.

GHOSTS   *las fantasmas*

old sheets
body part vocabulary
magic marker
newspaper
string

Children cut out a square of white material.
They crumple some newspaper and drape the material over it.
The head is tied with a string.
Children draw facial features on the material.

CALABAZA ENMIELADA

3 lb. piece of pumpkin (or marrow) cut into six pieces	la calabaza cortada
1 lb. brown sugar	azúcar moreno
6 tablespoons of water	cucharadas de agua
1/4 pint whipped cream	la crema batida
marashino cherries	las cerezas confitadas

Remove the seeds.	Quite las semillas.
Put/Arrange	Ponga/Arregle
Sprinkle	Rocie
Cover/Simmer	Cubra/hierva a fuego
Baste	Pringue

Remove the seeds from the pumpkin or marrow.

Put the water in a shallow oven-proof dish and arrange the pieces of pumpkin in it.

Sprinkle with the sugar and bring to a boil.

Cover the dish and simmer for an hour, basting with the syrupy liquid every 15 minutes.

When tender, allow to cool.

Arrange the pumpkin in dishes, pour the syrup over them, and top with whipped cream and maraschino cherries.

IMAGINATION

Teacher reads the following skit.

Children role-play the parts.

It can also be a feltboard story.

Characters:	**Props:**
boy	house
girl	moon with witch
black cat	sign saying Halloween
pumpkin	
bat	
ghost	
skeleton	

Once upon a time there was a boy and a girl.	Había una vez un muchacho y una muchacha.
They saw a house.	Los dos veían una casa.
They opened the door of the house. (make creaking sound, e-e-e)	Abrieron la puerta de la casa. (inhale making deep gutteral sound e -e -e)
They went inside.	Pasaron adentro.
To the right they saw a black cat (meow, meow) and they were afraid.	A la derecha veían un gato negro (miau, miau) y tenían miedo.
To the left they saw a pumpkin. (hissing sound for flickering candle)	A la izquierda veían una calabaza. (hissing sound for flickering candle)
They went up the stairs slowly.	Subían la escalera despacio.
Soon they saw a bat (wings fluttering; hook thumbs together and flit fingers) and they were afraid. (hands to mouth)	De pronto vieron un murciélago (wings fluttering; hook thumbs together and flit fingers) y tenían mucho miedo. (children put hands to mouth)

They continued going up the stairs and they saw a ghost. (Boo!)
Then they turned around and went downstairs quickly.
The passed the bat. (flit fingers)
They passed the pumpkin. (hiss)
They passed the black cat. (meow)
And they were afraid.
They opened the door and there in front of them was a skeleton. (click teeth together)
"Ay-ya-ya-yai!" they screamed.
They ran and ran and ran.
They fell to the ground.
They were breathing rapidly.
They looked at the sky and they saw the moon.
Soon they saw a witch passing the moon. (deep throaty cackle of witch)

But they were not afraid (boy and girl shake heads no) because they knew (nod heads yes) that it was Halloween night. (hold card up saying Halloween)

Seguían subiendo la escalera y veían una fantasma. (Boo!)
Entonces dieron la vuelta y bajaron la escalera rápidamente.
Pasaban el murciélago. (flit fingers)
Pasaban la calabaza. (hiss)
Pasaban el gato negro. (meow)
Y tenían miedo.
Abrieron la puerta y allí en frente de ellos estaba un esqueleto. (click teeth together)
—¡Ay -ya -ya -yai!— gritaron los dos.
Corrían y corrían y corrían.
Se cayeron al suelo.
Estaban respirando rápidamente.

Miraban al cielo y veían la luna.
De pronto vieron una bruja pasando por la luna. (deep throaty cackle of witch)

Pero no tenían miedo (boy, girl shake heads no) porque sabían (nod heads yes) que era el día de las brujas. (hold card up saying Halloween)

ALL SOULS DAY
el Día de los Muertos

Explain to the children that this day is celebrated much like Memorial Day in the United States. Graves are visited, picnics take place and food is made. Talk about Bread of the Dead and explain that while eating this special bread the family remembers those who have died.

Children love this activity.
They are fascinated by the crossbones.
They also enjoy the taste of the bread.
You may want to divide this recipe in two parts.
The teacher or one group does everything up to the asterisk.
Another group finishes.
The next day everyone can taste the bread.

BREAD OF THE DEAD

Pan de Muertos

From **Mexican Cookery**
©HP Books, Inc., Tuscon, AZ 85703
(602) 888-2150

Quaint dough sculpture decorates bread traditionally served on All Soul's Day.

1 cup milk	la leche
1/2 cup butter, softened	la mantequilla
1/2 cup sugar	el azúcar
1-1/2 teaspoons salt	cucharaditas de sal
1/2 teaspoon anise seeds, ground	la piel de naranja bien rallada, semillas molidas
1 envelope active dry yeast (1 tablespoon)	1 cucharada de levadura
Pinch sugar	un poco de azúcar
1/4 cup warm water	agua caliente
2 whole eggs	2 huevos enteros
3 egg yolks	3 yemas
1 teaspoon water	1 cucharadita de agua
5-1/4 to 5-1/2 cups all-purpose flour	la harina
2 tablespoons sugar	2 cucharadas de azúcar

Scald	Queme	*Divide	Divida
Pour	Eche/vierta	Set aside	Ponga a un lado
Stir	Revuelva	Shape	Forme
Cool	Enfrie	Roll	Enrolle
Knead	Amase	Bones	los huesos
Clean	Limpie	Moisten	Moje
Grease	Engrase	Press	Apriete
Cover	Cubra	Repeat	Repita
Dough	la masa	Sprinkle	Rocie
Baking sheet	el comal	Bake	Cocine al horno
Remove	Quite	Cool	Enfrie
Makes	Hace		

Scald milk by heating to just under boiling point, about 180°F (80°C). Pour over butter, 1/2 cup sugar, salt, orange peel and ground anise seeds in a large bowl. Stir until sugar is dissolved. Let cool. Stir yeast and pinch of sugar into 1/4 cup warm water. Let stand until yeast is softened. Beat whole eggs and egg yolks in a small bowl. Spoon 2 tablespoons beaten eggs into another small bowl or a custard cup. Stir in 1 teaspoon water. Refrigerate and use for glaze. Stir softened yeast and remaining beaten eggs into milk mixture. Stir enough flour into milk mixture to make a stiff dough. Turn out onto a lightly floured surface. Knead until smooth and elastic, at least 10 minutes, adding more flour as needed. Clean and grease bowl. Place dough in bowl, turning to grease all sides. Cover with a dry cloth towel. Let stand in a warm place free from drafts until doubled in bulk, about 1 hour. Punch down dough and turn out onto surface. Let rest while greasing 2 small baking sheets. Divide dough in half. Set aside about 1/3 cup from each half.* Shape large pieces of dough into smooth round loaves. Place on prepared baking sheets. Brush with some of reserved egg mixture. Divide 1 of the small pieces of dough into 3 equal pieces. Roll 2 pieces into 8-to 9-inch ropes. Shape ends of ropes to resemble knobs on bones. Cross bone shapes over top of one loaf, stretching to reach bottom of each side. Shape third piece of dough into a ball. Moisten bottom with egg mixture. Place in center of crossbones, pressing firmly. Repeat with remaining small piece of dough and remaining loaf. Cover loosely with towels. Let stand in a warm place until doubled in bulk, about 45 minutes. Preheat oven to 350°F (175°C). Brush loaves evenly with egg mixture. Sprinkle each loaf with 1 tablespoon sugar. Bake 30 to 35 minutes or until browned. Remove from baking sheet; cool on racks. Makes 2 loaves.

THANKSGIVING   *el Día de Gracias*

Practice please and thank you while passing out a special Latin food.

TURKEY   *el pavo*

ditto
crayons

Draw a turkey on a ditto.
Children color in the feathers of the turkey.

BELL BRACELETS   *las pulseras*

elastic cord
scissors
bells

Cut strips of elastic Christmas cord into 7″ strips.
Slip on bell and tie around child's arm.
Cord comes in red, silver, green, gold and blue.
Sing Jingle Bells with the children.

SONG
(Jingle Bells refrain)

Cascabeles, Cascabeles,
Vamos a cantar
Qué alegría
Todo el día
de la Navidad.

SONG
(Deck The Halls tune)

Navidad, navidad, tra, la, la, la, la, la, la, la, la.
¡Qué alegría, qué alegría, tra, la, la, la, la, la, la, la, la.
Todo el mundo canta, canta, tra, la, la, la, la, la, la, la, la.

CHRISTMAS TREE   *árbol de la Navidad*

ditto
crayons

Draw a Christmas tree with bulbs at the end of the branches on a ditto.
Label the bulbs. Children color in the appropriate colors.

GOD'S EYE   *Ojo de Dios*

yarn
glue
popsicle sticks
paper clips

This makes a simple Christmas ornament.
Glue two popsicle sticks together in the shape of a cross.
Wind the yarn over and under the sticks alternating as you go.
Children may want to change yarn colors to create a pattern.
Glue paper clip to the back of the stick for hanging.

CHRISTMAS EVE SALAD

Ensalada de Nochebuena
From **Mexican Cookery,** ©HP Books, Inc.
Tucson, AZ 85703, (602) 888-2150

A spectacular combination of fruits and nuts topped with ruby pomegranate seeds.

The beets give the salad a pink color.

However, my experience has been that many children don't like beets.

Therefore, you might mix in the beets for color and then place them along the sides of the salad for decoration.

Removing seeds from a pomegranate takes awhile. Allow extra time.

This is a tasty salad.

Use small dixie cups for sampling.

Peel	*Pela*	Shred	*Desmenuce*
Cut	*Corte*	Sprinkle	*Rocíe*
Dip	*Meta*	Blend	*Mezcla*

4 small beets	*remolachas pequeñas*
water	*el agua*
2 tablespoons sugar	*2 cucharadas de azúcar*
1/4 lb. jicama or 1 additional red apple	*una manzana*
1 orange	*una naranja*
2 to 3 tablespoons lime juice or lemon juice	*jugo de lima o limón*
1 red apple	*una manzana*
2 small bananas	*bananas pequeñas*
6 large romaine lettuce leaves, finely shredded	*la lechuga*
3 tablespoons roasted unsalted peanuts	*los cachuetes*
2 tablespoons pine nuts	*las nueces*
1/4 cup pomegranate seeds	*semillas de granada*
2 tablespoons sugar	*cucharadas de azúcar*
1/4 teaspoon salt	*cucharadita de sal*
3 tablespoons white vinegar	*el vinagre blanco*

Cut off beet tops, leaving about 1 inch of stems. Do not remove root. Scrub beets and place in a small saucepan. Add water to cover and 2 tablespoons sugar. Bring to a boil; reduce heat. Cover and simmer 45 minutes or until beets are tender. Drain and rinse with cold water. Rub off skins under cold running water. Refrigerate beets until serving time. Before serving, peel jicama and cut in thin small wedges. If using apple, leave unpeeled. Peel orange and cut in thin slices. Cut each slice in half. Place lime juice or lemon juice in a small bowl. Cut unpeeled apple into thin wedges. Dip each wedge in juice to prevent discoloration. Peel banana and cut into thin slices. Dip into juice. Cut cooked and peeled beets into thin slices. Line a broad shallow salad bowl with shredded romaine lettuce. Arrange jicama, orange, beet, apple and banana slices in alternating circles or other pattern on lettuce. Sprinkle with peanuts and pine nuts. Top with pomegranate seeds. In a small bowl, blend 2 tablespoons sugar, salt and vinegar until sugar is dissolved. Drizzle over salad just before serving. Makes 6 servings.

Variation:
Reserve cooking liquid from beets. Cut jicama, apple, orange, bananas and beets into small chunks. Combine with nuts and pomegranate seeds. Add dressing and enough beet liquid to color mixture a bright pink. Toss gently and arrange on romaine leaves. Serve immediately.

LAS POSADAS

Nine days before Christmas, on December 16, a procession begins in the streets of Mexico in which Mary and Joseph seek "posada" or a place to stay. Each night they are refused at the door until Christmas Eve. Then they are welcomed inside. Jesus is born. A piñata is broken to celebrate the event.

Do a short skit enacting "Las Posadas."
You will need:

9 children	(each holding a book in front of their face, representing a door)
Mary	(bathrobe and veil)
Joseph	(bathrobe, pillowcase over head tied around forehead with scarf)
3 Kings	(presents and Burger King hats)
3 shepherds	(same as Joseph)
1 donkey	(shawl or Mexican blanket over child on all fours)
2 sheep	(a tie-hat with cotton balls on face)
2 cows	(black circles around eyes and bell on neck)
2 candles	(2 children carrying candles lead procession)
1 baby doll	(Jesus in manger)
1 narrator	(introduces characters and reads story)
4 signs	(one says: 9 days before Christmas.)
	(one says: Is there room?)
	(one says: It's Christmas Eve.)
	(one says: Jesus is born.)

Our presentation is called "Las Posadas," with Mary, the mother of Jesus; Joseph, Mary's husband; the angels, the animals, the shepherds, and the three kings.

For nine days before Christmas Mary and Joseph go from house to house looking for a place to stay. At each door they ask if there is room. "There is no room." "Go away."

Now it is midnight. It is cold. It is the Holy Night, the 25th of December. Mary and Joseph arrive at a place and here Jesus is born. Joseph kisses Mary. Then he takes Jesus and puts him in a blanket. The angels sing. The animals watch. The shepherds pray. The kings bring gifts. The children sing: "Happy Birthday" to Jesus. Then they sing: "Jingle Bells." (Children can shake their bell bracelets here while singing.) Merry Christmas!

Nuestra presentación se llama —Las Posadas,— con María, la madre de Jesús; José, el esposo de María, los angelitos, los animales, los pastores y los tres reyes.

Por nueve días antes de la Navidad María y José van de casa a casa buscando posada. A cada puerta preguntan si hay posada. —No hay posada.— —Váyanse.—

Ahora es la medianoche. Hace frío. Es la Noche Buena, el 25 de diciembre. María y José llegan a un lugar y aquí se nace Jesús. José le da un beso a María. Entonces él tome Jesús y lo pone en una manta. Los angelitos cantan. Los animales miran. Los pastores rezan. Los reyes traen regalos. Los niños cantan: ¡Que los cumplas feliz! ¡Que los cumplas feliz! ¡Que los cumplas, Que los cumplas! ¡Que los cumplas feliz! Entonces cantan: —Cascabeles.— ¡Feliz Navidad!

THREE KINGS

el Día de los Reyes

Children in Mexico leave their shoes out on January 6 with hay and water for the king's camels. Their shoes are filled with little gifts. The day is celebrated much like Christmas in the U.S.

PIÑATA PARTY

Plan a party to celebrate the coming of the kings. Make or buy a piñata. To make a piñata you will need:

flour
water
balloons
pin
newspaper strips cut lengthwise

paint
tissue paper
scissors

Blow up the balloon.
Dip the newspaper strips into a mixture of flour and water.
Layer the strips over the balloon.
Allow to dry between applications.
Adorn the piñata with paint or tissue paper.
Hang piñata from ceiling.
Each child is blindfolded and gets a chance to strike open the piñata.

PAPER PLEASERS

tissue paper
scissors
clothesline

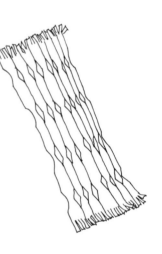

Use three sheets of tissue paper.
Cut the tissue paper into four parts.
Fold the tissue accordion style.
Fringe the ends with scissors.
Scallop the sides leaving space between each scallop.
Open the decoration and hang on the clothesline.

MARACAS

styrofoam cups
paint or crayons
dried beans
popsicle sticks
masking tape

Each child receives two styrofoam cups.
He then draws a design on his cups.
Several beans are placed inside the cups.
Place the two cups together at their openings.
Tape the cups together.
Insert a popsicle stick in the bottom of one of the cups.
Children shake maracas, chanting "Dale, Dale" as each child tries to break open the piñata.

VALENTINES DAY

el Día do los Amantes

Cut out pink hearts.
Write on the bottom of the heart:
"Kisses for you."   *Besos para ti.*
Child chooses either pink or red lipstick.
Paint their lips.
Child kisses the pink heart.
This is a great activity for pre-schoolers.
Even the boys enjoy the lipstick!

¿Me amas?
¿Me adoras?
¿Qué me das?
Un besito
nada más.

Have children make valentines.
This is a fun way to learn affectionate expressions in the language.
I love you.   *Te quiero.*
You are my love.   *Eres mi amor.*
How divine!   *¡Qué divina!*
A hug for you.   *un abrazo para ti*
dear, sweetheart.   *Querida*

VALENTINES

Jan Keenan
Scottville, MI

red paper
pencils
scissors

Teacher directs children:

Today is Valentine's Day.   *Hoy es el Día de la Amistad.*
We give a valentine to a friend.   *Damos una tarjeta a un amigo.*
Fold the red paper.   *Doblen el papel rojo.*
Draw part of a heart.   *Dibujen parte de un corazón.*
Cut the heart on the line.   *Corten el corazón por la linea.*
Write "I love you."   *Escriban —te quiero.—*
Give the valentine to a friend.   *Den la tarjeta a un amigo.*
Hug your friend.   *Abracen su amigo.*

CARNAVAL

water balloons   clothesline
candles   clothespins
rope   party favors
pillow cases   tissue paper
confetti

Carnaval is three days of pre-Lenten festivities, usually in February or March. It is
   characterized by dancing, masquerades and celebrating in the streets.

You may want to have a "fiesta" or party outdoors to celebrate "carnaval."
Children can dress up in costume for the events of the day.

A clothesline can be hung with small "jincanas" or party favors pinned to the line.
The packages may contain candy, cookies, small toys or amusing gifts like rice,
   feathers, or confetti.
One jincana is empty.
Children who have won a contest are blindfolded first.
Then they hit a package with a stick.
All other participants follow.

The following games from Peru can be played.

Water Balloon Toss.
During "carnaval" buckets of water are dropped from balconies onto passers-by.

Candle Race *(Carrera Velas)*.
Children run with lighted candles to a finish line without letting the candle go out.

Tug of War..

Pillow Case Race *(Carrera de encostalados)*.
Children hop to a finish line.

Tag *(La Serpiente)*.
All children that the chaser tags, hold hands to form a "snake."
They help him catch the other children.

The chaser is chosen like this:
One player holds out his hand, palm up and the other children place their index
   fingers into his open palm.
The player quickly closes his hand.
The child whose finger is caught becomes the chaser.

Confetti marks the end of the celebration.

*Tag is for about ten players.

FLAG DAY   el Día de la Bandera

construction paper
straws
stapler

February 24 is Mexican Flag Day.
Have children make a flag of Mexico by gluing together the appropriate colors,
   red, green and white.
Staple a straw to the side of the flag.
Have children march around chanting Viva Mexico, Viva Mexico!

EASTER   la Pascua

Make a decorative egg ditto.
Children color in.

EL GORDITO

Count on fingers with each "Este."
On "este gordito" lick the thumb and all the fingers.

This little boy found an egg;	*Este muchacho halló un huevo;*
This one cooked it,	*Este lo coció,*
This one peeled it,	*Este lo peló,*
This one salted it,	*Este le echó la sal,*
This fat little one ate it.	*Este gordito se lo comió.*

Cute rhyme for Easter time.
Adapted from **Tortillitas para Mamá,** by Holt, Rhinehart and Winston, 1981.

EASTER

gatito *ovejita*
perrito *pollito*

Easter means new life.
Show children pictures of kittens, puppies, lambs, chicks, etc. to illustrate "ito/a" ending of these words.

EGGS

plastic eggs
book

Play "huevos."
Three children at a time sit in front of the teacher.
Each child chooses one egg and hides it in his lap.
The teacher has not seen their choices.
The book is placed in front of the first child.

Child:	Knocks three times, saying:	*—tan, tan, tan.—*
Teacher:	Who is it?	*¿Quién es?*
Child:	It's __(child's name)__	*Es* _____
Teacher:	Do you have animals?	*¿Tiene animales?*
Child:	I don't have animals.	*No, no tengo animales.*
Teacher:	Do you have food?	*¿Tiene comida?*
Child:	I don't have food.	*No, no tengo comida.*
Teacher:	Do you have eggs?	*¿Tiene huevos?*
Child:	Yes, I have eggs.	*Sí, tengo huevos.*

Teacher has three guesses to determine what color child has.
The eggs are placed in two winning columns, one for the teacher, one for the child.

PAN AMERICAN DAY

Celebrates the formation of the Organization of American States in 1931.
See "Flags" under "Culture."

Children choose a country, make a flag and process around the room with their delegation on April 14.

MOTHER'S DAY   *el Dia de la Madre*

TISSUE FLOWERS

tissue paper
long pipe cleaners

Big tissue flowers can also be a gift on Mother's Day.
Give three or four sheets of tissue paper to each child.
Demonstrate how to fold the paper accordion style.
Place small pipe cleaner in center of folded paper and twist.
Separate, lift, bend, and fluff layers of flower to form petals.
The flowers can later be used to ornament the top of the Christmas tree.

YARN COLLAGE

ditto
pencils
construction paper
glue
yarn

Children make Mother's Day Cards and enclose a yarn artwork of flowers or birds.
The children address the outside of the card to:
Señora . . . (children should check to see what their mother's maiden name is so
they can address the full Spanish name) e.g. *Señora Meyer de Ervin.*

Teacher dittos a simple flower such as a tulip or a bird.
Children choose one item.
They fill the flower or bird with glue and wind the yarn into coils filling the entire
object.
If winding is too difficult for the younger children, they may precut several pieces
of yarn and simply apply them to the glue.

FATHER'S DAY   *el Dia del Padre*

BADGES

construction paper
pencils
crayons

Children can make Father's Day cards and enclose a badge to wear on Dad's shirt.
The children would address the outside of their card to *Señor . . .*
The badge would be made out of construction paper leaving space in the middle
to write . . . *Papá Felipe* or whatever Dad's name is.

BOOKS

Teacher explains sentences.
Children draw pictures.
Staple books.

May there always be sunshine.	*Que siempre sea luz del sol.*
May there always be blue skies.	*Que siempre sea cielo azul.*
May there always be Daddy.	*Que siempre sea papá.*
May there always be me.	*Que siempre sea yo.*

CHAPTER IV
Tips For Teachers

The following tips and comments for teachers can apply to classrooms of toddlers through teens.

DO plan your presentation. Anticipate how the children might respond. Think about how you will handle discipline problems or lack of comprehension. Teaching plans should respond to a particular situation and the needs of the children. Flexibility is important. Plan how an activity will be introduced, developed and its objective. Evaluate the results before the next group time.

DO come to class prepared. While using the command form seems easy, it takes preparation. You can go through a series of commands in a matter of minutes and are then left without enough material for the remaining class time.

DO use a crescent shaped seating arrangement where possible. This allows the children to see each other and teacher demonstrations more easily. This seating arrangement contributes to a more informal environment and enhances the child's ability to relax.

DO display posters, menus, signs, vocabulary words, cultural items and maps. Change them regularly. Children will absorb this peripheral information effortlessly.

DO sell the program to the staff and parents. The more support you enlist the more credibility your foreign language program will have.

DO speak Spanish or other target language as much as possible.

DO respect the children through your attitude, the way you speak to them and your general demeanor.

DO tell the children about the format of the class; what they can expect to happen next.

DO reward the children for good attitudes, behavior and participation. (Children love foreign language stickers, stars, a nod of approval, a touch or a smile)

DO wear native clothing or jewelry now and again to class.

DO let the children know where they are going and what they have learned. (Use videotape or simple evaluation games, i.e. recognition, draw, do it, what is this, search out answer.)

DO proceed slowly with new vocabulary. Too much at once cannot be retained.

DO allow the child to reverse roles with the teacher, i.e. he commands class to perform certain actions.

DO appreciate the child, his sense of wonder, curiosity and playfulness. Present new material in novel and interesting ways.

DO accept the new language as it is spoken. Criticism of mistakes in speech will not alleviate the problem. However, hearing more language which the child can understand will improve his speech.

DO vary activities and pace to keep the child alert. A very small child (2-1/2 - 3 yrs.) can be attentive for only 5 to 10 minutes. Quiet activities followed by large motor activities is a good rule of thumb.

DO proceed from the simple to the complex, i.e. command form, first person (I dance), third person (he dances), teacher reads story to class, (they and we dance) and finally conversation and description.

DO present material in interesting ways:
Directions: Scratch my back to the right, to the left, up, down, in the middle.

Body Parts

Each child has a paper body part. The child is then blindfolded and tries to pin the body part on a large paper body. Children discover where their picture landed on the body.

DO encourage conversation and description. A simple method is:
Use three piles of cards, i.e. colors, nouns, and opposites or nouns, actions and places. Child chooses one card from each pile. He then composes a creative sentence using vocabulary from all three piles, i.e.
The **cow** is **big** and **black**.
The **mother eats** in the **kitchen**.

DO relax your discipline habits. TPR can be referred to as a spectator sport because the whole class is watching, learning and anticipating a response to the teacher's command. The noise level may increase as more participation takes place.

Rules

Be courteous and respect everyone.	*Sea cortés y respete a todos.*
Sit correctly.	*Siéntese correctamente.*
Listen and pay attention.	*Escuche y ponga atención.*
Raise your hand if you want to speak.	*Levante la mano si quiere hablar.*
Speak in a low voice.	*Hable en voz baja.*
Don't scream.	*¡No grites!*

DO include the foreign language evaluation on the report card. A sample evaluation form is below:
In the foreign language class, your child:

☐ is progressing satisfactorily
☐ is doing well
☐ is doing very well
☐ seems to enjoy the class
☐ shows enthusiasm, motivation
☐ has a positive attitude
☐ sets a good example for others
☐ is attentive
☐ actively participates in class activities
☐ is putting forth best effort
☐ exhibits self control
☐ shows confidence in guessing meaning or connection of words
☐ has good comprehension
☐ uses Spanish to converse, to imitate teacher
☐ can associate written word to spoken word

☐ is distracted easily
☐ has poor comprehension
☐ seeks attention through disruptive behavior
☐ interrupts others by talking out of turn
☐ needs to speak louder
☐ could participate more
☐ does not participate
☐ has ability to do better
☐ needs extra help to catch up with the rest of the class
☐ lacks interest in foreign language experience
☐ prefers large group, small group activities

DO keep a master list of vocabulary that the children are hearing including shadow words, on a roll of paper towel or notebook.

DO keep a notepad near your bed at night. As you teach foreign language in novel ways, ideas will abound during the day but especially at night. Write them down for future use.

DO practice patience with the children. Allow time for the child to touch and observe interesting objects. Give him time to respond orally, being careful not to answer for the child if he knows the answer. Communication can be a joyful and frustrating experience for a child. But joy and frustration are necessary ingredients to independence, self esteem and fluency.

DO model good language, pronunciation and diction. When the child says, for example, "What Daddy do?" you might say, "Oh, what is Daddy doing?" and then answer the question.

Some fun simple pronunciation exercises are as follows:

VOWELS

Son cinco vocales,
a, e, i, o, u.
Son cinco niñitas
Lindas como tú.
Van siempre juntas
a, e, i, o, u
Son cinco niñitas
Lindas como tú.

LISTEN

Alumno
Elefante
Iglesia
Octubre
Uno

CHEERS

Give me an "e"   *elefante*
Give me an "s"   *sol*
Give me an "p"   *perfecto*
Give me an "a"   *animal*
Give me an "ñ"   *niño*
Give me an "o"   *oso*
Give me an "l"   *libro*

What does it spell?
¿Qué deletrea?   ¡Español!

I SPY

Teacher:
I see, I see   *Veo, veo*
Class:
What do you see?   *¿Qué ve usted?*
Teacher:
A little thing   *Una cosita*
Class:
What little thing is it?   *¿Qué cosita es?*
Teacher:
Something that begins with.... *Algo qué empieza con....*

TONGUE TWISTERS

La mar estaba serena
serena estaba la mar

Yo te daré
te daré
niña hermosa
te daré
una cosa
una cosa
qué yo solo sé
. . . café

erray con erray
cigarro
efay con eray
ferrocarril

Brinca la tablita,
Yo ya la brinqué,
Brinca la tablita,
Ya ya me cansé.
(Repeat)

Lentes, lentes
No son dientes.

Chucu -loco
Chucu -tora
Chucu -lo locomotora
Chucu -ferro
Chucu -ril
Chucu, chucu, chucu, chucu
Vamos en ferrocarril.

Perro, perrito,
Perro, chiquitito.
Perro, perrito,
Perro, chiquitito.

Sombrero, sombrero
No es bolero.

PAT-A-CAKE

This is a chant sung in Spain much like "pat-a-cake."
Children pair off.
They tap first their partner's right hand, then his left on the rhyming part.

On street	En la calle -lle
twenty-four	veinte cuatro -tro
there was	ha sido -do
an assassin.	un asesinato -to.
An old woman	Una vieja -ja
killed a cat	mató un gato -to
with the point	con la punta -ta
of her shoe.	del zapato -to.
Poor woman.	Pobre vieja -ja.
Poor cat.	Pobre gato -to.
Poor point of the shoe.	Pobre punta -ta del zapato -to.
The old woman	A la vieja -ja
they jailed.	le encarcelaron -ron.
The cat	al gato -to
they buried.	lo enterraron -ron.
The point of the shoe	A la punta -ta del zapato -to
they threw	lo tiraron -ron
in the river.	en el barranco -co.

DO use index cards for lesson planning. A simple format for teaching the Total Physical Response method is as follows:

REVIEW (old vocabulary)
INTRODUCE (new verbs, vocabulary)   PROPS _____
COMMANDS (actual recipe or lesson)
RECOMBINATION (Point to Tom with the banana)
CLOSING (song, farewell to teacher and children)
*Note that the commands and recombination parts of the sequence constitute actual practice in the language.

DO keep the target language meaningful, i.e.

ordering and eating a meal in a restaurant.

trying on clothes, buying them and packing a suitcase.

dialing a number and talking on the telephone.

visiting the doctor.

following directions: make a meal, a craft, a card, a gift, running errands, an obstacle course, etc.

DO make the children work. They can provide their own supplies, i.e. scissors, crayons, pencil, baggies, glue stick, ruler, notebook, props from home. The children can help you make materials, i.e. bingo boards, go fish cards, flashcards, etc. Attendance is mandatory.

DO send home a monthly newsletter apprising the parents of what their children are doing in school. The more interest you develop in the program the more help you will get in promoting it.

DO collect regalia from garage sales, wish lists sent home, pre-school and early elementary materials, children's stuffed animals, toys, house and farm accessories and the dimestore.

DO save catalogs, magazines, National Geographics.

DO encourage a show and tell time in the classroom.

DO expect the best from the children which includes attendance, behavior in class and participation.

DO review often to ensure success for the child. Children do not tire of repetition if it serves a purpose. REVIEW. REVIEW. REVIEW.

DO recombine the vocabulary the children are acquiring. Recombination is a combination of words that the children have not heard in a particular sequence. Recombination will create comradery, interest and enthusiasm for what you are doing. Some examples are listed below:

Point to Tom with the banana.

Take the lion and jump.

Touch the fork with the spoon.

Put the mittens on your feet and walk.

Dance with the monkey.

Eat with your toes.

Throw a shoe in the soup.

Draw purple hair on the lion.

Eat the hot dog with the knife.

Put the tiger in the refrigerator.

DO include shadow words (my, your, the, a) in a command. The children will acquire them effortlessly.

DO allow the child to demonstrate his taste for language, i.e. counting ability, special books in the target language which he wishes to share with the class, souvenirs from trips, etc.

DO solicit help from the parents in providing interesting experiences for the children, i.e. cooking, art, dance, music, artifacts, or slides from travel.

DO encourage parents to purchase books, dictionaries, records or tapes to reinforce the foreign language commitment.

DO contact local high schools and request speaking engagements from visiting exchange students.

DO use the informal form (*tú*) with small children if you are more comfortable with it.

DO use the following common expressions:

Sit like an Indian.	*Siéntese como un indio.*
Look at me.	*Míreme.*
Speak in Spanish.	*Hable en español.*
Stand in line.	*Pónganse en fila.*
Don't run.	*No corren.*
Walk.	*Caminen.*
Wait your turn.	*Espere su turno.*
Silence.	*Silencio.*
Please.	*Por favor.*
Thank you.	*Gracias.*
Very good.	*Muy bien.*
Perfect.	*Perfecto.*
Repeat.	*Repiten.*
in a loud voice	*en voz alta*
in a soft voice	*en voz baja*
again.	*otra vez*
faster	*más rápido*
slower	*más despacio*
Come in.	*Pase.*
Come here.	*Venga aquí.*
An applause, please.	*Un aplauso, por favor.*
Time to go.	*Ya es hora.*
Congratulations.	*Felicitaciones.*
Bless you.	*Salud.*
I like that.	*Me gusta eso.*
It is pretty/beautiful.	*Es linda/bella.*
How nice you are.	*¡Qué simpático eres!*
Are we friends?	*¿Somos amigos?*
What does this mean?	*¿Qué quiere decir . . .?*
Tell me, what is . . .	*¿Dígame, qué es . . .*
What do you need?	*¿Qué necesita usted?*
Who wants a turn now?	*¿Quién quiere un turno ahora?*
Is it your turn?	*¿Es su turno?*
Where is . . .	*¿Dónde está . . .*
How are you?	*¿Cómo está usted?*
Why are you sad?	*¿Por qué estás triste?*

DO leave a TPR activity for a substitute teacher. The activity may include directions that the children can follow to complete a craft, project, etc. Tapes and TPR commands which review past vocabulary are other alternatives in the teacher's absence.

DO incorporate music into the teaching of foreign language. For older children you may wish to type some simple phrases in both languages on a ditto. Baroque music (Handel or Bach) is played while the children listen to the phrases being read by the teacher in the foreign language. The teacher turns the music off and repeats the phrases. The music is on again and the children are listening to the teacher read the phrases. The music is off and the children fold the paper down the middle and translate the phrases silently.

DO NOT be undermined by staff members who do not understand the second language acquisition process and right brain approaches such as TPR and suggestopedia. Show them what the children know, invite them in, let them experience children tasting language.

DO NOT be too predictable in the presentation of commands to the child. Children will automatically respond before the command is given if they anticipate a particular sequence.

DO NOT use English. Try to use the target language as much as possible. The more foreign language is heard the better the chance that it will be acquired.

DO NOT expect all children to be interested in a foreign language. Keep the children guessing so as to enlist their attention and cooperation.

DO NOT treat the child disrespectfully. Rapport between the teacher and the child is essential to a positive early foreign language experience. Use "please" consistently.

DO NOT get discouraged by the child's rate of progress. Children absorb language at different speeds. Look for what they have acquired since the week or month before.

DO NOT directly correct mistakes in speech or pronunciation. Rather, model the child's response correctly, i.e. Daddy go? Teacher: Oh, where did Daddy go? Overt correction does not guarantee success the next time. However, hearing the spoken language often and in context from a fluent speaker will provide the necessary input to the child for reproducing the language efficiently and fluently.

DO NOT hesitate to provide more information or explanation so that the child can understand more clearly the language he is hearing.

DO NOT present formal grammar lessons until much later. Remember, native American children hear English for 6 or 7 years before being introduced to grammar. We are concentrating on communication and content not form and grammar.

DO NOT stay on one activity too long. Pacing and variety is important to maintain the child's attention and cooperation.

DO NOT use language lab without using picture books simultaneously. See Harris Winitz under "Resources," or the Learnables in this chapter.

The following resources are tasty tricks for children.

ENGLISH CARD

Spanish or other target language is spoken as much as possible. Anyone found speaking English is given the English card. At the end of class those children holding the English card must perform an action decided upon by fellow classmates.

PHOTO CUBE

Insert picture cards into a plastic photo cube or post-it paper cube for vocabulary review of nouns, adjectives and verbs. Children throw the cube like dice and identify the picture facing up.

SHADE

Use a cloth shade to draw a family tree. Roll down the shade as needed. Simple to store.

HANGMAN

Introduce the alphabet through a game of Hangman. Child thinks of a word and tells the teacher privately. Teacher draws the blanks needed to complete the word on the chalkboard. Class guesses which letters are in the word. For each incorrect guess the teacher draws the features of a man one by one until he is hanged. Children love this game.

WORD SEARCH

Hide several words in a maze of letters on a ditto. Children circle the vocabulary either up, down, across or diagonally. Use only words which the children have heard before.

PASSWORD

Teacher writes a vocabulary word across the chalkboard. Children think of any number of words corresponding to each letter of the password, i.e. —*tomate*— (tomato)

t	o	m	a	t	e
techo	octubre	Mamá	Adiós	Tomás	elefante

CUES

On your vocabulary flashcards draw a pink bow in the corner for feminine words and a blue bowtie for masculine words. This cues the child as to which article to use with the word.

TRIVIAL PURSUIT

Children love board games. Use miniature cars or colored markers to proceed around the board. Teacher prepares some simple vocabulary words which the children have heard in class. Child turns the card over, translates it, rolls the dice and proceeds around the board. If he lands on a space with a circle he may have another turn. First child around the board wins.

Some sample cards are outlined below:

a yellow square	*un cuadrado amarillo*
friends	*amigos*
five fingers	*cinco dedos*
two girls	*dos muchachas*
The pepper is black.	*La pimienta es negra.*
a skinny father	*un padre flaco*
Open your mouth.	*Abra la boca.*
the right hand	*la mano derecha*
the hamburger	*la hamburguesa*
It's hot.	*Hace calor.*
the pants	*los pantalones*
Put on the blouse.	*Póngase la blusa.*
Scratch your stomach.	*Rásquese el estómago.*
brown shoes	*zapatos marrones*
a fat mother	*una madre gorda*

a big house	*una casa grande*
number 15	*número quince*
number 45	*número cuarenta y cinco*
number 120	*número ciento veinte*
It's 5:30.	*Son las cinco y media.*
jinglebell	*cascabel*
two small eggs	*dos huevos pequeños*
Take off the hat.	*Quítese el sombrero.*
on top of the table	*encima de la mesa*
Monday	*el lunes*
fried eggs	*huevos fritos*
two windows	*dos ventanas*
Touch your foot.	*Tóquese el pie.*
hot	*caliente*
blonde hair	*pelo rubio*
brown hair	*pelo castaño*
two circles	*dos círculos*
It's cold.	*Hace frío.*
Give me a kiss.	*Déme un beso.*
an orange blouse	*una blusa anaranjada*
Run.	*Corre.*
Stop.	*Párese.*
under the plate	*debajo del plato*
cold milk	*la leche fría*
March.	*Marche.*
Turn around.	*De la vuelta.*
Stand up.	*Levántese.*
Close your eyes.	*Cierren los ojos.*
February	*febrero*
three crayons	*tres creyones*
Point to the blackboard.	*Apunte a la pizarra.*
the left arm	*el brazo izquierdo*
Touch your chest.	*Tóquese el pecho.*
a long line	*una linea larga*
around the chair	*alrededor de la silla*
the desk	*el pupitre, el escritorio*
Walk forward.	*Camine hacia adelante.*
Walk backward.	*Camine hacia atrás.*
a door	*una puerta*

AUDIO CARD READER

Vocabulary can be supplemented in the classroom by a tutorette machine which
   employs magnetic picture cards and earphones.
This machine is for individual use.
Pictures can be drawn or glued on the cards.
Stickers of animals, for example may also be placed on the cards.

PICTURE DICTIONARY

Teacher prepares alphabet pages for each child.
When the child knows a variety of vocabulary and has heard it used in the
classroom he can then begin to record the words in his dictionary.

Page letter "A" in Spanish might have three pictures , *abeja* (bee), *árbol* (tree), and
abuelo (grandfather)
Each picture is numbered.
Six blanks from one to five are also numbered on the page.
The teacher writes a word in the first blank, i.e. *abeja* or bee, preceded by the
article, —*la.*—
She writes the articles for the other pictures.
Children fill in the remaining blanks with words.
A creative sentence can then be supplied by the child which pertains to any one of
the vocabulary words for that letter of the alphabet.

Aa

1. _la abeja_
2. _el_
3. _el_
4. _____
5. _____
6. _____

Escriba una frase.

PUPPETS

Describe what the teacher is doing, comment, or ask questions of the puppet:

Teacher:	I dance.
Puppet:	You dance?
Teacher:	Yes, I dance.
Puppet:	You dance very well.
Teacher:	Thank you, I dance good and fast.
	What do I do?
Puppet:	You dance.
Teacher:	Yes, I dance.

SHOWER CURTAIN

A beautiful world map is printed in color on a shower curtain.
The curtain is available from Jacobson's or the United Nations.
The shower curtain can be used for Twister games of colors and countries.

LINGO GAME

An inexpensive food bingo game is available from UNICEF. See "Resources."
You can also make your own bingo boards using pictures from *The Practical Vocabulary Builder* by National Textbook Company.

LEARNABLES

Harris Winitz of International Linguistics Corporation, has developed a series of picture booklets which accompany tapes. The content of the picture booklets increases in complexity as the child's listening ability progresses. This system is a powerful tool for second language acquisition and has a number of uses. A couple of applications are outlined below.

The teacher describes the pictures on a page in the booklet.
Each picture is numbered.
The teacher then asks where on the page does it say such and such.
No writing is involved.

Later, the teacher asks what is picture no. 3.
The child says what is happening.

TOOLS

Other miscellaneous tools of the trade are pictures from coloring books, greeting cards, story books, puzzles, dot-to-dot drawings, flannel boards, magnetic numbers and letters for magnetic chalkboard.

ANIMAL FUN

Plastic noses of various animals are popular now. Have a child select a nose, put it on and the class identifies which animal he is.

DITTOS

Teacher draws a rabbit or other figure on a ditto.
Child tells teacher seven or eight words that he knows in the target language.
Teacher writes them inside the rabbit for take-home.

Teacher places Spanish words on or near items in the classroom.
Child completes a ditto which says: I found these Spanish words in my classroom.
They mean . . .

CHAPTER V
Comments For Bilingual Parents

Jane Merrill in her book, **Bringing Up Baby Bilingual,** writes of successfully meshing a busy life with a second language and raising twins. There are common themes running through her practical experience which were also found in other bilingual families. My research from completed questionnaires of bilingual parents revealed the challenges and satisfactions derived from passing on a second language to one's children. Several tips and comments can be gleaned from the questionnaires and bilingual parents such as Jane Merrill.

Introducing a second language to your children requires a **commitment.** You must become conditioned to teaching a foreign language at home. Words are carefully chosen for dialogue with young children just as you would do in your native language. Living bilingually places an extra demand on children. However, children emotionally identify with the second language because they have grown up with it. It has been a family custom or ritual as it were.

Bilingual families are characterized by an inner security. There is a sense of family destiny about this special gift. Bilingualism forms an extra bond between family members. The bilingual family has a strong personality. Rituals, jokes and warm, intimate occasions abound.

Bilingual children develop a sensitivity and love for language. They are unusually attuned to verbalizing definitions of words. The bilingual child feels proud of his knowledge. He feels in charge. He is an authority translating for a third party. Bilingual children are comfortable at storytelling. Their reports to an audience are interspersed with both languages. The children even critique their parents.

Bilingualism at home requires **confidence.** There are controlling moments when a child speaks back in English. Steer the conversation back into the second language. Parents early on will be inclined to use English to praise or reprimand a child. Remember that language must precede emotional responses.

Practicing a second language requires **discipline.** Keep in mind that the use of a second language will peak and subside according to the degree of exposure. Maximize exposure to the second language.

A bilingual commitment is revealed through the purchase of books and records. Plan ahead for emerging interests such as geography (toy globe), cooking (native cookbook) or if reading, (picture dictionaries.)

Acquiring a second language has many benefits and gives children another window on the world; a new way of seeing things. There are many ways to do things; all are fine. A new language brings culture, sensitivity and understanding as a young child. Early bicultural family experiences develop an appreciation for parents and their role in the family.

Using a second language at home necessarily involves challenges. One challenge that bilingual parents encountered was peer influence. Some bilingual teens preferred their parents not use the second language when their friends were visiting. Other parents having children attending Saturday schools in the Washington D.C. area noted that their children did not use the second language with their friends. Learning a second language was a family priority and experience.

As children approach junior high and high school their peers and school activities may interfere with the foreign language objective. Switching to another language after having spent a full day in school can be hard. One parent recounts that as school involvement became more pronounced in extracurricular activities, more and more English was spoken at home. The children were excited to explain their new activities and did so increasingly in English.

Another parent was concerned about the transition of her children to pre-school. But, she recounts, the children were proud of their language ability, especially when she came to the classroom to teach what her children already knew.

Another challenge presented itself if one parent was not bilingual. In this situation, the child had a means to control the parents through linguistic ploys.

Societal insensitivity to bilingual families can present yet another challenge. Older children may be embarrassed to use the language outside of the home.

Know that these challenges need not become obstacles to second language acquisition in the home. As has been noted, confidence, commitment and discipline will make the difference in a successful second language experience in the home.

See For Yourself

Bilingual children use the second language in solitary play. They sing songs and fluctuate in both languages while playing with trucks and dolls.

You will see your child master color names for example, in the second language, before English.

You will see your child use the language with relatives. Endearments and affectionate terms will be spoken spontaneously.

You will see with what ease children switch from one language to another. One bilingual parent recalls an incident involving her son, age 5. His grandmother was visiting and she spoke poor English. The grandmother was having trouble understanding her daughter's neighbor, who had a thick brogue. Very gently, the grandson, who was playing next to the women, turned to his grandmother, translated what the neighbor was saying into French and went back to playing.

You will see children apply what they have learned to the real world. On passing a pond, one child asked his bilingual parent why the duck didn't quack in French like the one on the record. A bilingual teacher recounts of her experiences speaking Spanish in the classroom, in the hallway and all through the school. When the English speaking children noticed their teacher still speaking Spanish after class, they remarked, "Poor teacher, she doesn't know English," and they used the Spanish expression, —Pobrecita— to express their dismay.

You will see the child surpass you. He will bring language to the family from other sources.

Your bilingual child can be a well-integrated person. He is a coveted precious national resource. He will score higher than matched monolinguals on IQ tests. He will be able to distinguish shades of meaning across languages. An early second language experience will enable your child to acquire other languages more easily. Being bilingual offers your child an opportunity to become more self-confident, open-minded and intellectually enriched.

The following tips should help you on your way:

DO have a positive attitude and enthusiasm for your mission. It will go a long way to building the necessary rapport needed for an enjoyable bilingual experience.

DO introduce the second language in as natural and spontaneous a manner as possible.

DO make the foreign language experience a pleasant, recreational time together.

DO use commands, repetition, listening, songs, games and books for practical language experience.

DO refrain from correcting grammar mistakes. Model good language and the child will absorb and reproduce it fluently over time.

DO search for the meaning which the child wishes to convey.

DO coin words or give descriptive names to items which are nonexistent in the target country.

DO stay in the target language. Invent words or talk around a missing word.

DO reward the child for speaking in the second language.

DO learn discipline words in plenty of time to use them.

DO cook and eat ethnic foods.

DO celebrate holidays; continue religious and cultural traditions.

DO place dictionaries around the house. They will become friends to the child.

DO choose your words carefully to ensure full comprehension by the child.

DO purchase materials to enhance teaching at home.

DO read to your child in the second language. The investment in books and dictionaries will reflect your commitment.

DO respect the child. If a teen is uncomfortable with speaking a second language in front of his peers do not force him to do so. Compromise and respect can co-exist successfully. Find a time that is mutually satisfactory to both of you.

DO expect challenges along the way. Anticipate and plan accordingly. These challenges need not impair your foreign language objective.

DO get together with other people who speak the language your child is acquiring. That way he will know that other people understand him. Some parents have even hired bilingual babysitters from nearby colleges to entertain and care for their children.

DO set aside some time every day for special games, songs, etc. as a special treat for your child.

DO make the child feel proud of knowing more than someone else through positive reinforcement.

DO involve the family in travel to the country, exchange programs, pen pal writing or cultural events.

DO NOT permit the insensitivity of society or the negative attitude of others to influence your decision to pass on a second language.

DO NOT revert back to English if stuck on a word. Try to convey meaning with other vocabulary.

DO NOT believe that by introducing a second language early in life the child will be behind in English language skills. Children can acquire two languages simultaneously with enormous benefits. Linguists tell us that two languages do not confuse a child. However, the child may take a little longer to start talking. Cognitive skills are definitely enhanced by acquiring two languages at once.

DO NOT allow the child to control or defeat your purpose. A positive attitude, compromise and commitment are essential to successfully using a foreign language in the home.

CHAPTER VI
Resources

This chapter will help to streamline your work at home or school by providing a wealth of practical information. The chapter is divided into five parts. They are:

Resources
Professional Journals
Materials
Books for Children
School Observations

Enjoy these tools for teaching.

RESOURCES

ACTFL (American Council on the Teaching of Foreign Languages), Inc.
P.O. Box 408
Hastings-on-Hudson, NY 10706

publishes *Foreign Language Annals* and provides listings of current materials.

Second Languages and the Basics, available from ACTFL

a useful public relations brochure promoting the value of second languages.

El Arte Culinario Mexicano, available from ACTFL

easy to prepare recipes available in Spanish and English.

Foreign Language in the Elementary School: State of the Art, available from ACTFL

foreign language instruction, theory and practice.

ALL (Advocates for Language Learning)
P.O. Box 4964
Culver City, CA 90231

quarterly newsletter informing parents and teachers of issues in second language acquisition.

Center for Applied Linguistics
1118 22nd St., N.W.
Washington, D.C. 20037

research and application.

DORS to Language
44 Morningside Drive
Tiffin, Ohio 44883

monthly newsletter packed with ideas and information about second languages.

ERIC Clearinghouse on Languages and Linguistics
1118 22nd St. N.W.
Washington D.C. 20037

runs searches of the ERIC database for researchers and educators in foreign languages and linguistics. It also supplies mini-bibliographies on specific topics such as:

Involving Parents in Bilingual Education Programs, April 1985
Small Group Work in the Language Class, January 1986
Teacher Attitudes in the Second Language Classroom, August 1984
Research on the Relationship between Children's First and Second Language Learning, November 1986
Suggestopedia, May 1985
Vocabulary and Second Language Learning, September 1985

- articles from the bibliographies can be read in libraries with an ERIC collection or ordered from:

> EDRS, Computer Microfilm International Corp.
> 3900 Wheeler Avenue
> Alexandria, VA 22304

Fifty-Fifth St. School Spanish Immersion Program 2765 S. 55th St. Milwaukee, WI 53219	provides handbook and cassette of: **Helping Parents Learn a Second Language with their Children.**
Information Center on Children's Cultures U.S. Committee for UNICEF 331 East 38th St. New York, NY 10016	provides cultural and bibliographic information on specific countries around the world.
Iowa FLES Newsletter 300 Pearson Hall Iowa State University Ames, Iowa 50011	newsletter for teachers of foreign language in the elementary school.
The LIND Institute Box 14487 San Francisco, CA 94114	teacher training workshops on accelerated learning.
Lozanov Learning Systems, Inc. 1315 Apple Avenue Silver Spring, MD 20910	accelerated learning
Michigan Foreign Language Newsletter Western Michigan University Languages and Linguistics Kalamazoo, MI 49008-3899	advertisements, current events
Northeast Conference on the Teaching of Foreign Languages P.O. Box 623 Middlebury, VT 05753-0623	advertisements, articles, tips and reviews.

Professional Journals

Foreign Language Annals
Hispania
Language Learning
Modern Language Journal

MATERIALS

Alemany Press 2501 Industrial Pkwy, West Hayward, CA 94545	**The Children's Response** (short TPR activities) **The Natural Apprpach** (theoretical work)

Acquisition through Creative Teaching: The Artful Use of Suggestion in Foreign Language Instruction
Center for Continuing Development
64 Mountain Street
Sharon, MA 02067

practical experience applying suggestopedia in the classroom

Alpha Plus Foreign Language Systems, Inc.
P.O. Box 3323
Edmond, Oklahoma 73083

Hablan los Niños by Bishop (Teacher's manual) and other materials

Berty Segal, Inc.
1749 Eucalyptus St.
Brea, CA 92621

TPR workshops and activity books

The Bilingual Family: A Handbook for Parents by Edith Harding and Philip Riley, Cambridge University Press

Bowmar, Inc.
4563 Colorado Blvd.
Los Angeles, CA 90030

elementary school Spanish classroom materials

Bringing Up Baby Bilingual
Facts on File
460 Park Ave. S.
New York, NY 10016

Jane Merrill, 1984
comprehensive book about the bilingual experience

Conversational Spanish for Children: A Curriculum Guide
Iowa State University Press
2121 South State Ave.
Ames, Iowa 50010

outlines the sequence of tenses used in conversational practice

Dale Seymour Publications
P.O. Box 10888
Palo Alto, CA 94303

about 12 books in the series provide the artwork for topics like Funny Folks, Cartoon Zoo, Holiday Helps, School Events, Shopping Spree and Sports World

Dairy Council of Northern Indiana
501 E. Monroe
South Bend, IN 46601

set of food punch-outs
(contact your local dairy council)

Discovery Toys

good pre-school and school products that can be adapted for language class. Contact hostess in your area.

D'Va Illustrated Cards
1496 Parkhill Rd.
Cleveland Heights, OH 44121

verbs, adjectives, food, clothing, clocks, etc.

A FLES Sampler: Learning Activities for Foreign Language in the Elementary School: FLEX, FLES and Immersion

G.C. Lipton, Ed., available from: American Association of Teachers of French, 57 E. Armory
Champaign, IL 61820

Frank Schaeffer Publications, Inc.
26616 Indian Peak Rd.
Rancho Palo Verde, CA 90274

Gessler Publishing Co., Inc.
900 Broadway
New York, NY 10003-1291

Handbook for Planning an Effective Foreign Language Program, 1985
Publications Sales
California State Department of Education
P.O. Box 271
Sacramento, CA 94802-0271

Hap Palmer Music
Educational Activities, Inc.
P.O. Box 392
Freeport, NY 11520

Hear N' Tell Adventures
320 Bunker Hill Rd.
Houston, Texas 77024

¡Hola! Vamos a Cantar
Shawnee Press, Inc.
Waring Drive
Delaware Water Gap, PA 18327-1099

HP Books, Inc.
P.O. Box 5367
Tucson, AZ 85703

International Linguistics Corporation
401 West 89th Street
Kansas City, Missouri 64114-0697

Judy Company
4325 Hiawatha Ave. S.
Minneapolis, Minnesota 55406

The Kiosk
19223 DeHavilland Drive
Saratoga, CA 95070

Magnetic Way
2495 North Forest
Amherst, New York 14068

McGraw-Hill Book Co.
School Division
P.O. Box 25308
Oklahoma City, OK 73125

Michigan Products
1200 Keystone Ave.
Box 24155
Lansing, MI 48909-4155

Siguiendo Instrucciones
and other ditto masters for use with small children

Topical ditto masters with instructions, i.e. "Color the pants brown." Request **Juego de Colores.**

outlines a comprehensive program to initiate, implement and evaluate foreign language acquisition.

records and tapes

children's folk stories accompanied by tapes, flashcards and game boards

songbook and record, short 2-4 line songs

Mexican Cookery

The Learnables (tapes and picture booklets) by Harris Winitz

wooden puzzles for children

interesting native games and boards

magnetic board and overlays of real life scenes

language development cards; good for topical vocabulary (Group B)

audio card reader mentioned in Chapter IV

National Textbook Company
4255 West Touhy Ave.
Lincolnwood, Illinois 60646-1975

Basic Vocabulary Builder I and
Practical Builder II; topical ditto
masters good for bingo exercises

First Start in Spanish by Myriam Met
available from National Textbook Co.

teacher's manual for
elementary school

Sky Oaks Productions, Inc.
P.O. Box 1102
Los Gatos, CA 95031

Dr. Asher's TPR manual, other
practice books plus classroom aides
and films

Speak Spanish to your Baby
Chou-Chou Press
P.O. Box 152
Shoreham, NY 11786

easy phrases to use; by
Therese Slevin Pirz
(available in French also)

Springboard to Foreign Language
available from:
The Language School
YMCA Building
909 Fourth Ave.
Seattle, WA 98104

Michael Olaf
The Montessori Shop
5817 College Avenue
Oakland, CA 94618

special books, cookbooks, puzzles,
games and materials

Teach Me Tapes, Inc.
P.O. Box 35544
Minneapolis, Minnesota 55435

music tapes for children with words
accompanied in booklet

**Um, Um, Oh, Oh or How to Communicate
in a Foreign Language**
1005 Debra Lane
Madison, WE 53704

idea book by Monica Severa;
available from SUMO Publishers

BOOKS FOR CHILDREN

The First Thousand Words in Spanish
International Book Centre
P.O. Box 295
Troy, MI 48099

picture book available in five other
languages at specialty stores

¿Eres tú mi Mamá?
Random House, New York, 1973

story by Dr. Seuss

Barron's Educational Series, Inc.
113 Crossways Park Drive
Woodbury, NY 11797

Season books (4 in series)
Senses books (5 in series)
Los Padres (The Parents)

Los Tres Osos
LTO Enterprises
6036 N. 10th Way
Phoenix, AZ 85014

children's stories

¿Cómo Se Llaman?
Midwest European Publications, Inc.
915 West Foster St.
Evanston, IL 60201

story books and comic books

Troll Associates
320 Rt. 17
Mahwah, NJ 07430

small, one-line, illustrated pages;
easyreader books such as:

Feliz Cumpleaños (Happy Birthday)
Un Dinosauro en Peligro (verbs: to sleep, to wake up)
Una Función de Títeres (Animals)
Samuel el Espantapájaros (Halloween)
Un Carro de Bomberos Grande y Rojo (Professions)
Contento Juan (Food)
¡Listos, en sus Marcas, Adelante! (verb: to run)

• The above books are good to read with related vocabulary in parentheses).

Tortillitas para Mamá
Holt, Rhinehart and Winston
New York, 1981

Hispanic nursery rhymes

**Doña Blanca and other Hispanic
Nursery Rhymes and Games**
T.S. Denison & Co., Inc.
Minneapolis, Minnesota, 1983

Recommended School Observations:

Cincinnati Public Schools
230 E. 9th Street
Cincinnati, OH 45202

Contact: Nelida Mietta-Fontana

*Ferndale Public Schools
881 Pinecrest
Ferndale, MI 48220

Contact: Lynn J. Haire

Milwaukee Public Schools
P.O. Drawer 10K
5225 W. Vliet St.
Milwaukee, Wisconsin 53201-8210

Contact: Helena Anderson-Curtain

*all kinds of materials including picture dictionaries, picture flashcards, etc. are for sale at very reasonable prices.

See: **Foreign Language in the Elementary School: State of the Art,** Center for Applied Linguistics, for a listing of schools in the U.S.

BIBLIOGRAPHY

Asher, James J., 1986, **Learning Another Language through Actions: The Complete Teacher's Guidebook,** Sky Oaks Productions, Inc., Los Gatos, CA

Ashworth, Mary and Patricia Wakefield, 1982, "Teaching the Non-English Speaking Child: Grades K-2," Center for Applied Linguistics, Washington, D.C.

Barrio, Constance García, 1986, "How to Teach Your Baby a Second Language, *American Baby* magazine, March issue.

California State Dept. of Education, 1985, **Handbook for Planning an Effective Foreign Language Program,** Sacramento, CA

Dhority, Lynn, 1984, **Acquisition through Creative Teaching: The Artful Use of Suggestion in Foreign Language Instruction,** Center for Continuing Development, Sharon, MA

Dulay, Heidi and Marina Burt and Stephen Krashen, 1982, **Language Two,** Oxford University Press, New York

García, Ramiro, 1985, **Instructor's Notebook How to Apply TPR for Best Results,** Sky Oaks Productions, Los Gatos, CA

García, Rebecca and Sue Reynolds, "Foreign Language Teacher's Attitudes: A Strategy for Exploration and Change," *Foreign Language Annals,* Vol. 10, No. 6.

Glisan, Eileen W., "Total Physical Response: A Technique for Teaching All Skills in Spanish," *Foreign Language Annals,* Vol. 19, No. 5.

HP Books, Inc., **Mexican Cookery,** Tuscon, AZ

Joiner, Elizabeth G., "Listening from the Inside Out," *Foreign Language Annals,* Vol. 17, No. 4

Krashen, Stephen D. and Tracy Terrell, 1983, **The Natural Approach,** Alemany Press, Hayward, CA

Levy, Yonata, "Theoretical Gains from the Study of Bilingualism: A Case Report," *Language Learning,* Vol. 35, No. 4

Linse, Caroline, 1983, **The Children's Response,** Alemany Press, Hayward, CA

Merrill, Jane, 1984, **Bringing Up Baby Bilingual,** Facts on File, New York

Met, Myriam, "Elementary School Foreign Languages: Key Link in the Chain of Learning," Center for Applied Linguistics, Washington, D.C.

Met, Myriam, "Listening Comprehension and the Young Second Language Learner," *Foreign Language Annals,* Vol. 17, No. 5

Pirz, Therese Slevin, 1985, **Speak Spanish to Your Baby,** Chou-Chou Press, Shoreham, NY

Rhodes, Nancy and Audrey Schreibstein, 1983, "Foreign Language in the Elementary School: A Practical Guide," Center for Applied Linguistics, Washington, D.C.

Rosenbusch, Marcia Harmon and Ann María Graber, 1982, **Conversational Spanish for Children,** Ames, Iowa

Schaefer, Dolores A., "My Experiences with the Lozanov Method," *Foreign Language Annals,* Vol. 13, No. 4

Schinke-Llano, Linda, 1985, **Foreign Language in the Elementary School: State of the Art,** Center for Applied Linguistics, Washington, D.C.

Schneider, Judith Morganroth, "PTA and TPR: A Comprehension Based Approach in a Public Elementary School," *Hispania,* Vol. 67, No. 4.

PRONUNCIATION GUIDE

Pronunciation in Words	Letters of Alphabet	Pronunciation of Letters	Practice
ah	a	ah	abril, carta, capitán
b, **v**	b	beh	bebé, li**b**ro, bolsa
ss, **hard c**	c	seh	cesta, **c**on, bici**c**leta
ch	ch	cheh	chocolate, curro, echar
d, **th**	d	deh	donde, dinero, e**d**ificio
e	e	eh	empanada, enero, escritorio
f	f	eh-feh	teléfono, favor, fuego
gut. h, hard g	g	hey	**g**ente, segundo, co**g**er
silent h	h	ah cheh	Hondoras, hora, hoy
ee	i	ee	iglesia, primero, ridículo
throaty h	j	hoh-tah	joya, Jorge, reloj, ejemplo
*k	k	kah	kilo, kilómetro
l	l	eh-leh	lunes, lápiz, algo
substitute y for ll	ll	eh-yeh	amarillo, llama, estampilla
m	m	eh-meh	diciembre, mes, miércoles, mamá
n	n	eh-neh	nada, nubes, nuestro
ny	ñ	eh-nyeh	año, otoño, baño
o	o	oh	octubre, ocho, noche
p	p	peh	perfecto, papel, padre
*k	q	koo	quiero, que
r	r	eh-reh	Ricardo, rojo, Eduardo
trill the r	rr	eh-rreh	ferrocarril, perro, carrera
ss	s	eh-seh	sistema, sol, sábado
t	t	teh	tarde, tiempo, científico
oo, **kweh**	u	oo	útil, autobús, **cue**ro
soft b	v	beh	vez, evidentemente, voz
*w	w	dob-bleh-veh	(words having "w" use "v" instead.)
z, **s**	x	eh-kees	Xochimilco, e**x**plicar
y, **ee**	y	ee-gree-yeh-gah	yo, ayer, **y**
ss	z	seh-tah	zona, cabeza, zapato

- The Spanish language is very phonetic. It sounds as it reads.
* The letters K and W are not of Spanish origin.

Accents mark unexpected stress of differentiated word meaning: si (if) and sí (yes).

The **last** syllable is stressed in words ending in a consonant: animal (ah-nee-MAHL)

The **second to last** syllable is stressed in words ending in a vowel: mesa (MEH-sah)

ABOUT THE AUTHOR

Mary Jo Ervin has taught Spanish to children and adults in both public and private settings. She has taught in the fields of education and business. Her work experience, in addition to teaching, ranges from bilingual secretary and service representative for Ford Export Division to student and ambassador of good will. In 1974 she was awarded a Rotary International Foundation fellowship. She attended la Universidad Católica in Córdoba, Argentina. *She has visited Mexico, Colombia, Ecuador, Peru, and Argentina. Mary Jo is an accomplished public speaker and active in community service. She resides in Howell, Michigan with her husband and three daughters.*